HOW TO MAKE THE RIGHT CAREER MOVES

Deborah Perlmutter Bloch, Ph.D.

VGM Career Horizons
a division of *NTC Publishing Group*
Lincolnwood, Illinois USA

Acknowledgments

My appreciation goes to my friends and colleagues who shared their observations and expertise on the aspects of career development presented in this book.

My husband was, as always, an essential provider of specific knowledge and general support.

Author's Note: The names of all individuals and companies and the addresses and phone numbers used in examples and samples in this book are fictional.

Library of Congress Cataloging-in-Publication Data

Bloch, Deborah Perlmutter.
    How to make the right career moves / Deborah Perlmutter Bloch.

        p.   cm.
    ISBN 0-8442-6664-7 (soft) : $7.95
    1. Career development.   2. Job hunting.   I. Title.
HF5381.B465   1990
650. 14—dc20   90-32816
                                                                                    CIP

1991 Printing

Published by VGM Career Horizons, a division of NTC Publishing Group.
© 1990 by NTC Publishing Group, 4255 West Touhy Avenue,
Lincolnwood (Chicago), Illinois 60646-1975 U.S.A.

1 2 3 4 5 6 7 8 9 VP 9 8 7 6 5 4 3 2

Contents

Acknowledgments ii
About the Author v
Foreword vii
Introduction ix

Section I: Where I Am Today

1 **How Am I Doing? 2**
How Employers Evaluate Job
Performance 3
Job Performance Rating Criteria 9
Evaluate Your Own Job
Performance 13

2 **Sometimes I'm Happy . . . 19**
How Satisfying Is My Current
Job? 20
What Is Most Important to Me? 24
Next Move—Up, Across, or Out? 39

Section II: Where I Will Be Tomorrow

3 **Moving Ahead Right Here 44**
Setting Goals for Self-Improvement on
the Job 45
Seeking and Getting a Raise 58
Getting Promoted 63

4 **Moving Out—How to Find the
Right Job 68**
Should I Move Out? 69
Where Do I Want to Go? 71
How Do I Get There from Here? 76

5 **Making Your Résumé Work 84**

Tips from Employers on Winning Résumés 85
Beginning the Writing 86
Rewriting for the Reader's Attention 99
Producing a Perfect Finished Résumé 102
Writing a Cover Letter 106
Tracking the Results of Your Résumé 108

6 Winning Interviews 111
Assess Your Strengths and Weaknesses 112
Learn about the Job 116
Match Your Skills to the Job 118
Give the Right Answers 123
Ask the Right Questions at the Right Time 125
Turn Nervous Energy into Positive Energy 130
Track the Results of Your Interviews 131
Extra Tips for a Winning Interview 133

7 How to Make the Right Career Moves—A Final Word 136

Appendix A: Consumer Guidelines for Selecting a Career Counselor 141

Appendix B: Related Readings 144

About the Author

Deborah Perlmutter Bloch, Ph.D., is an associate professor of educational administration at Baruch College, the City University of New York. Previously, she worked as the Director of MetroGuide, New York City's computer-based Career Information System; and before that as the Coordinator of Research for the Office of Occupational and Career Education of the New York City Board of Education.

As a consultant, Dr. Bloch has worked for the National Career Information System at the University of Oregon, the Departments of Education and Labor of New York State, and the Iowa Department of Economic Development.

Dr. Bloch has served as an officer and director of the National Career Development Association (NCDA), the American Vocational Association Guidance Division, and the Association of Computer-Based Systems for Career Information. She has published many articles in professional and popular magazines and given numerous presentations and workshops for counselors and teachers on how to help people with their career decisions and job search. She is the author of three previous books about career development, and she is the president-elect of NCDA.

Foreword

Has your career come to a standstill in terms of challenge and advancement? Are you wondering whether you're in the right job, the right company, or even the right field? Would you like to give your career a boost that gets you moving upward once again? If your answer to any of these questions is "yes," then this book is for you.

How to Make the Right Career Moves gives solid, useful information and tips on getting your career back on track. The author is an acknowledged authority on career guidance and placement, and she draws on her years of experience to help you help yourself. Ms. Bloch's previous books with VGM on résumé writing, interviewing, and getting your first job have all helped thousands of people seeking to better themselves in the world of work.

We hope this new book helps you keep your career moving upward so that you may achieve the utmost in career satisfaction.

The Editors
VGM Career Horizons

Introduction

Now is the time to make the most of your career. This book will help you determine where you now stand in your career, where you would like to go, and how to get there. In other words, this book tells you *how to make the right career moves.*

For most of us, our jobs are central to our lives. We spend more than half our waking hours getting ready to go to work, performing on our jobs, thinking about how we have performed, or considering what we should do next.

Our jobs affect the most central aspects of our lives. Our jobs determine where and, to some extent, how we live. Day-to-day events on the job affect our relationships with people outside it. When things go right—or wrong—on the job, we often bring our feelings home, and those feelings about people and events on the job are reflected in how we react to family and friends. Most important, there is the sense of satisfaction we can get from work. When there is that overall sense of satisfaction, that feeling of having achieved a goal or contributed to a success, we feel good about ourselves. This book will help you determine if you are in the right job for you at this time in your life. If you are in the right job, it will help you identify your sources of satisfaction and learn how to maximize them. If you are not in the best job for you right now, it will help you figure out where and how to move to give you the satisfaction you want in your career.

A few words about terms used in this book. When we talk about *jobs*, we are talking about a particular position in a particular organization. When we use the word *occupation*, we mean all the jobs that are the same regardless of the organization. When we use the word *career*, we mean all of the jobs any one individual has held and the path he or she has taken moving from job to job and possibly from occupation to occupation.

For example, Sandy Tracks began work selling advertising space over the telephone. The job was telephone salesperson for Media Moguls. Sandy liked some things about the job and disliked others. Some of these things, like vacation policy and health benefits, had to do with the company, Media Moguls. But other things, like talking to many different people in a day and competing to raise results, had to do with the occupation of salesperson. When Sandy decided to move from Media Moguls to Space Cadets, it was a job change but not a change of occupation. When Sandy moved from sales to market analysis it was a change not only of job but of occupation. All of these jobs, whether in one occupation or several and whether within one organization or many, made up Sandy's career. This book is about how to make the right career moves, and that could include finding success in your current job or occupation, changing jobs, or even changing occupations.

How to Make the Right Career Moves is divided into two major sections. Section I, "Where I Am Today," sets the foundation for your career moves to success. It will help you understand both how your employer judges your performance and how you evaluate your current job. Section II, "Where I Will Be Tomorrow," will help you move to the next stage of your career through information on improving your current job performance and on successfully changing jobs.

In section I, there are two chapters. Chapter 1 asks the question "How am I doing?" and provides information directly from employers on job performance evaluation. Managers in companies ranging from huge multinational corporations to small partnerships from a variety of industries told us exactly how employees are rated and raises are determined. You will be able to evaluate yourself using the same kinds of checklists and forms that your managers use. Chapter 2, "Sometimes I'm Happy . . . ," helps you evaluate the job you currently hold, both in terms of the occupation you are in and the organization for which you work. You will examine the factors that are associated with satisfaction and dissatisfaction. Through checklists and questionnaires, you will be able to figure out whether your next career move should be a promotion in the company for which you currently work, to another job, or even to a different occupation.

In section II, "Where I Will Be Tomorrow," there are five chapters designed to help you put into operation the decisions you reached as you evaluated your performance and your job in section I. Chapter 3, "Moving Ahead Right Here," provides strategies for improving your job performance, getting a raise, and moving up in the organization in which you currently work. Chapter 4, "Moving Out— How to Find the Right Job," helps you answer the question "Where do I want to go?" and provides information on resources for occupational and job change ranging from working with headhunters to using computer systems. Chapter 5, "Making Your Résumé Work," summarizes the best tips from employers on writing and designing a winning résumé. It includes worksheets to help you begin your writing and samples to help you get a perfect finished copy. Chapter 6, "Interviews for Success," gives you techniques for interview preparation and presentation that will ensure effective job interviews. Chapter 7 provides a final word on making the right career moves.

Throughout *How to Make the Right Career Moves,* there are worksheets and tips to help you use the book easily in a way that is meaningful to you. The book concludes with a list of additional reading related to suggestions made in each of the chapters.

There is tremendous variation in the career paths that people follow. Some people begin their education knowing what they want to do and spend their careers doing it. However, more often, people change occupations during their careers. If you think about the plans you had for your work life in high school or college, you may see that you are doing something quite different from what you expected. With advances in technology and continual changes in the needs of society, previously unthought of opportunities occur or, it may seem, are thrust upon us. This book is written with the belief that we can shape our careers through self-examination combined with an understanding of the world of work. It is written in the hope that it will enable the reader to increase her or his capacity for self-examination, to add to her or his store of knowledge, and to bring the two together.

WHERE I AM TODAY

How Am I Doing? 1

We would all like to have the gift to see ourselves as others see us, to know whether other people really understand how much we bring to our work, to know whether they value our efforts as much as we do, even to know whether they see the same areas for improvement that we sense for ourselves. Knowing how others see us on the job, particularly when those others are responsible for rating us on our work, is particularly important because it can help us see whether there will be opportunities for advancement. This chapter is designed to help you see yourself on the job from your company's or organization's point of view.

The information in this chapter comes directly from managers who are responsible for evaluating employee performance and granting raises. The managers work for companies ranging in size from a two-person partnership employing ten people to a subsidiary of a large multinational corporation. They include people working in accounting, advertising, computer systems, hotel management, insurance, and sales. Their comments may be applied to almost all industries and occupations. You can use what they told us about how they evaluate employees to make judgments about your own performance.

This chapter has three parts. In the first part, the kinds of systems that many organizations use to rate people are described. The second part includes the kind of criteria used for rating and what these criteria mean. The third part is a rating guide for you to use to evaluate your own job performance.

How Employers Evaluate Job Performance

Many companies have regular annual or semiannual performance reviews which include granting raises. In these performance reviews, there are usually opportunities for the immediate supervisor to rate the employee, for that supervisor to discuss the rating with other managers, and for the employee to provide feedback or reactions to the rating. The rating process usually includes the identification, either formally or informally, of needed areas of improvement.

One of the managers described the process his company follows this way.

Job evaluation procedure 1

There is a formal yearly evaluation, and your raise depends upon that evaluation. There is also a half-yearly evaluation to help you identify action steps—to bring you up to speed. A lot of people hate evaluations, but mine are done to help so that when the formal yearly evaluation comes, there are no surprises. Before the evaluation, I give the employee the review form, and we both fill it out separately. Then we meet to compare them. If they are different, then I try to use data such as client letters or my own observations to help the employee see what has to be changed.

Every month after the first evaluation, I try to say things to jog people's memories of what they are supposed to do. The first month, I might say, 'I don't want you to answer this, but how are you doing on some particular goal we set?' By the second month, if I haven't seen the improvement myself, I might say, 'Well, show me what you've been doing.' When I review an employee, attitude is very important to me. Are you a team player? How do you relate to people within the department? How do you relate to people in other departments? This is very important because our work affects people in every other department. Of course I'm interested in production and in your techniques—how you go about doing the job.

Raises are directly tied to the ratings on the form. A 3 gets more than a 2, and so on. An average raise has recently been about 5 percent a year. If you are wonderful, you might get only 6 percent, which could be a little discouraging. If someone is really good, I will go to bat for her or him for more money.

Another company has a different process with more frequent evaluations based on each project or assignment. This is how a partner in the company described it.

Job evaluation procedure 2

We have a formal evaluation procedure that is supposed to take place after each project is completed. There are different forms depending upon the level of work. The supervisor of a project fills out the appropriate form immediately after the project is completed. Just before each raise period—there are two per year—the personnel director averages the ratings for each employee. If everyone is doing the job right, there might be eight to twelve evaluations per person per year. However, these project ratings are not always done as they should be—right after the completion of a project—and not as much attention is paid to these numbers as to the place on the bottom of the form for comments. Since different supervisors rate differently, it's often hard to compare the numbers, but the comments at the bottom of the forms are really critical. The comments are used to identify areas in need of improvement as well as highly commendable activities. The personnel director is supposed to show the ratings to the employee.

The compensation committee meets twice a year. It discusses each person's work, and each member of the committee makes a recommendation for a raise. If there is tremendous divergence in recommendations, it is discussed further. Usually the committee defers to the partner most involved with the employee. Then the partners meet with the people they supervise to tell them their raises.

Raises are based on the worth of the employee to the company and to the marketplace. We know what levels of salary are out there for people with similar training and ability. We try to see who has made the greatest contribution or shows the most potential. If you don't get a raise in our company, it really means you should leave.

You can see that this company has more formal procedures than others. While you might think that larger companies use more formal procedures than smaller ones, that is not always true. One administrator for a multinational Fortune 1000 company said there was no procedure in her company for anyone below managers. However, another company, in fact a very small one, supplied information on its evaluation process.

Job evaluation procedure 3

We have an employee handbook that we give to each new employee. It spells out the reviews. There is a performance evaluation six months after the hire date, a salary review one year after the hire date, and each year thereafter. The immediate supervisor completes the evaluation form, and the managers discuss it. The immediate supervisor then discusses the evaluation with the employee. The most important things we look for are dependability, cooperation, current job performance compared to past performance, job performance compared to others in the department, growth within the job, and growth within the organization.

There is a direct relationship between the performance evaluation and raises. We take the numerical rating and manipulate that with the cost-of-living increase and time on the job to come up with a percentage raise.

One final company policy we will look at combines several features we have already seen. These policies are carried out in a very large organization with people doing diverse jobs such as secretarial work, computer systems design, selling, and accounting. The same process and the same forms are used for all employees, including managers.

Job evaluation procedure 4

Salary raises are given each year in February after a review in January. However, the major performance review takes place in June or July. First, the major responsibilities of the employee are listed on the form. Then the manager is asked to evaluate the strengths and weaknesses demonstrated in accomplishing the responsibilities according to certain standards such as job knowledge, quality of work, and communication. There are eight of these categories for everyone and five others for all but clerical personnel. Finally, the manager gives an overall rating. With each numeric rating category, there is space for comments. I usually don't make comments unless the rating is unsatisfactory or the employee is really terrible. The rating also has a place for indicating career growth potential of the employee in this corporation. After the managers prepare the form, we schedule conferences with all the employees and give them copies of it. We go over the items, point by point, discussing the recommendations and getting feedback. Then the employee keeps the form overnight to make comments on it and sign it.

Individuals' raises are based on the ratings, but there is one "pot" for the department, so there is some negotiation. In addition to the base pay raise, there is usually incentive compensation. This year, for example, the "pot" for base pay raises was 5 percent and for incentive compensation, 20 percent. Of course some people got more of that "pot" and some less depending upon their performance.

In most organizations, rating employee performance seems to be done on a regular basis with set procedures. At times, these procedures are spelled out; other times, they seem to be determined by custom. Become familiar with the procedures in your company. Here are some questions to ask yourself about performance review procedures in your organization.

Performance Review Procedures in My Organization

1. What employee handbook or other document (if any) spells out the performance review procedures or times?

_____

_____

2. How often is the performance review carried out?

_____

_____

3. Who is responsible for rating my performance?

_____

_____

4. In addition to my immediate rating officer, who participates in reviewing my performance?

_____

_____

_____

5. What criteria are used to rate my performance?

_____

_____

_____

_____

_____

_____

6. What additional materials about my performance on the job are kept in my personnel folder?

_____

_____

7. What rights do I have to see the material in my personnel folder?

_____

_____

_____

8. Are there any company rules or procedures on the kinds of material or items to include in my personnel folder?

_____

_____

_____

9. When are raises usually considered and granted?

_____

_____

_____

10. What relationship is there between the performance evaluation and the raise?

_____

_____

_____

Job Performance Rating Criteria

Knowing the methods and procedures that companies use for evaluation is helpful, and so is knowledge of their rating criteria. When you examine rating criteria presented in this portion of the chapter, you can see what many organizations consider important in their performance evaluations. You can then mentally translate that into the criteria that apply to your job.

It is interesting to look at a number of rating forms, not because they are different but because they are so much alike. Many of the forms stress relationships with colleagues, supervisors, members of other departments, and clients of the organization. Many focus, as well, on growth, development, and improvement. Of course they all include areas related to specific job knowledge and productivity, but that is just one aspect on which you are being rated.

Some companies use evaluation forms that include broad, general criteria. Because these criteria are broad, they can be used to evaluate a wide variety of activities and behaviors. Because they are general, they can be used to evaluate people in a variety of jobs. The supervisor or rating officer has to apply the criteria, thinking of the specific responsibilities carried out by the employee. On each item, the employee is rated using a scale ranging from 1 for unsatisfactory to 5 for outstanding. Here are twenty items and their definitions taken from several companies' rating scales. The first thirteen items can be used to evaluate performance in just about any job. Items 14 through 20 apply more directly to your job if you have some role in managing the work of others.

Twenty items for rating job performance

1. Job understanding—Possesses a clear knowledge of the responsibilities and tasks to be performed.

2. Job knowledge and technical ability—Knows not only what needs to be done but how to accomplish the task; keeps abreast of new developments.

3. Quality of work—Produces concise, accurate work; takes pride in job responsibilities, output, and results.

4. Quantity of work—Meets necessary standards of output within a particular time frame.

5. Expense control—Operates effectively within budget constraints; seeks lower cost alternatives.

6. Listening skill—Uses information from the oral communication of others.

7. Oral communication skill—Expresses ideas in individual or group situations in a flexible manner to secure acceptance or agreement from listeners.

8. Communication—Possesses effective verbal and written skills; keeps co-workers, subordinates, and superiors informed; readily shares information.

9. Dependability—Completes assignments in the time specified; is available for suggestions and follows through as required.

10. Cooperation—Works willingly with associates, subordinates, supervisors, and others to achieve common goals.

11. Initiative—Makes active, self-generated attempts to achieve goals and influence events.

12. Innovativeness and creativity—Develops more effective and/or efficient approaches to projects; encourages new ideas and procedures; can quickly adapt to changing environments.

13. Judgment—Recognizes problems and evaluates priorities; makes appropriate decisions; makes effective use of time.

14. Problem analysis—Analyzes pertinent data properly; creates clear pictures of the current and proposed situations; is able to implement an effective plan.

15. Planning—Sets realistic and consistent objectives; reviews and updates plans and priorities based on changing demands.

16. Organization—Determines appropriate assignments of self and personnel and allocation of time and resources; coordinates activities of own personnel with those of others to achieve interrelated goals.

17. Delegation—Utilizes subordinates effectively; allocates information gathering, decision making, and other responsibilities to appropriate subordinates.

18. Development of staff—Motivates others and encourages teamwork; develops the skills and capabilities of subordinates through training, coaching, and rewarding positive performance.

19. Leadership—Uses varied interpersonal styles and methods in a flexible manner to guide individuals

or groups toward the completion of a task, the accomplishment of a goal, or the acceptance of a specific idea.

20. Decisiveness—Makes decisions, renders judgments, or takes action without hesitancy. Stays with a plan of action in spite of disappointment until a desired goal is reached or cannot be reached.

Some companies prefer to use forms with some general and some more specific items. For example, a marketing and sales division of a major hotel chain includes a number of the criteria in the first list but adds some items directly related to sales. Here is a list of ten of the items.

Ten items for rating sales performance

1. Product knowledge
2. Knowledge of the competition
3. Prospecting ability
4. Use of customer profiles
5. Ability to identify customer needs
6. Negotiating skills
7. Overcoming objections
8. Use of marketing plan
9. Telephone techniques
10. Rate quoting

Another example of specific criteria can be seen by looking at the items evaluated by a public accounting company. Again, these are in addition to more general items.

Five items for rating accounting performance

1. Knowledge of the client's accounting system
2. Knowledge of federal, state, and local tax laws
3. Adherence to accounting standards
4. Workpaper presentation (cross referencing, proper filing, etc.)
5. Acceptability by client

If you were being evaluated by a company that used the more general scale, you would still be rated on your specific abilities and performance. However, the rating would be incorporated under one of the categories such as "job understanding" or "job knowledge and technical ability."

Some other rating forms use short, easily understood phrases. Here is a list of commonly used rating items.

Fifteen phrases for rating job performance

1. Adjusts to new situations
2. Works with little or no supervision
3. Completes assignments within allotted time
4. Follows instructions
5. Completes work accurately
6. Asks intelligent questions
7. Shows interest in work
8. Communicates effectively
9. Cooperates
10. Accepts criticism
11. Demonstrates reliability
12. Demonstrates general ability
13. Shows potential for advancement
14. Demonstrates leadership qualities
15. Makes own decisions

Evaluate Your Own Job Performance

You will now have the opportunity to evaluate your own behavior on the job. Three rating worksheets are provided for this evaluation. The first rating scale is for general abilities that are expected on virtually every job. The second is for responsibilities unique to your job. The third is for your use if you have any managerial responsibility, that is, if you oversee the work of one or more other people.

When you evaluate yourself, you need to be as objective as possible. Think about how your behavior on the job, your performance, looks to others, not what is hidden within you. If you never come out with the original ideas that are inside your head, for example, you will have to rate yourself low on initiative. The only way people at work know you is through what you say and do. Use these evaluation sheets to rate what others can see.

In addition to being objective about your behavior on the job, you need to rate yourself, at this point, as you actually are, not as you would like to be. In chapter 3, you will be able to use the rating guide to help you figure out how to improve your job performance.

For each of the rating worksheets, use the following scale to rate your performance:

1 = poor or well below average

2 = fair or below average

3 = satisfactory or average

4 = good or above average

5 = excellent or outstanding

Rating Worksheet 1—Overall Job Performance

	Criteria	**Rating**
1.	Job understanding—I understand clearly the responsibilities and tasks of my job.	1 2 3 4 5
2.	Job knowledge—I know how to do my job well.	1 2 3 4 5
3.	Quality of work—I am proud of the work I produce.	1 2 3 4 5
4.	Quantity of work—I produce as much or more work as others in my job or department.	1 2 3 4 5
5.	Expense control—I operate within the time, money, or other resources allotted.	1 2 3 4 5
6.	Listening skill—I can follow instructions or information from others delivered orally.	1 2 3 4 5
7.	Oral communication skill—I feel comfortable expressing my ideas in planned or informal meetings.	1 2 3 4 5
8.	Written communication skill—My memos and letters to others are clear and complete.	1 2 3 4 5
9.	General communication—I share information with my subordinates, superiors, and fellow workers.	1 2 3 4 5
10.	Responsibility—I complete assignments in the time specified.	1 2 3 4 5
11.	Cooperation—I work well with associates, subordinates, supervisors, and others to achieve common goals.	1 2 3 4 5
12.	Creativity—I find new ways to get things done better and communicate them to others.	1 2 3 4 5
13.	Initiative—I work on my own to get things done.	1 2 3 4 5
14.	Judgment—I make decisions that work out well for the department or company.	1 2 3 4 5
15.	Adaptability—I can adjust to new situations.	1 2 3 4 5
16.	Independence—I can work with little or no supervision.	1 2 3 4 5
17.	Reliability—I follow work instructions and company policy.	1 2 3 4 5
18.	Motivation—I show interest in and enthusiasm for my work.	1 2 3 4 5
19.	Attitude—I accept criticism and see it as a way to improve my work.	1 2 3 4 5
20.	Leadership—I can often persuade others to do things in a better way.	1 2 3 4 5

Scoring: Add the numbers circled for each item. A perfect score is 100. You can consider your evaluation on the scale *Excellent* if you scored between 90 and 100. Your score is *very good* if you scored between 80 and 89. Between 70 and 79, consider your work *satisfactory*. If your score is between 60 and 69, it is *minimally satisfactory*. Below 60, your work is *unsatisfactory* or *poor*.

_____

Total Score

Rating Worksheet 2—Specific Job Performance

Directions: To complete this rating worksheet, you need to do a little more work. Before you can give yourself a rating, you need to identify the five most important responsibilities of your job. You can do this by thinking through what you do in a given day or week. You can also see if there is a job description prepared by your organization for your job. If there is, you may have a copy, or you may be able to get one from the personnel department. Another way to tackle this is to list all the job duties that you think are important and then discuss them with a co-worker in a similar position to figure out which five are most important. When you have identified five key job duties, list them in the spaces below and rate yourself, using the same scale, on each one. Be sure you do not omit a particular area of your job because it is not your favorite. Responsibilities you like least may be the most important ones for you to focus on.

Criteria	Rating
Job responsibility 1 _____	1 2 3 4 5
_____	
Job responsibility 2 _____	1 2 3 4 5
_____	
Job responsibility 3 _____	1 2 3 4 5
_____	
Job responsibility 4 _____	1 2 3 4 5
_____	
Job responsibility 5 _____	1 2 3 4 5
_____	

Scoring: Add the numbers circled for each item and multiply the total by four. A perfect score is 100. You can consider your evaluation on the scale *excellent* if you scored between 90 and 100. Your score is *very good* if you scored between 80 and 89. Between 70 and 79, consider your work *satisfactory*. If your score is between 60 and 69, it is *minimally satisfactory*. Below 60, your work is *unsatisfactory* or *poor*.

_____

Total Score

Rating Worksheet 3—Managerial Performance

Directions: An effective manager would score well on the first two rating worksheets as well as on the specific items of this rating worksheet. Use the same rating scale again.

Criteria	Rating
1. Leadership—I can guide individuals or groups toward the completion of a task, the accomplishment of a goal, or the acceptance of a specific idea in a variety of ways.	1 2 3 4 5
2. Problem analysis—I can analyze pertinent data correctly and create a clear picture of proposed solutions.	1 2 3 4 5
3. Problem solution—I can decide upon and implement an effective plan to solve problems.	1 2 3 4 5
4. Planning—I set realistic and consistent objectives.	1 2 3 4 5
5. Flexibility—I review and update plans and priorities based on changing demands.	1 2 3 4 5
6. Delegation—I involve personnel at all levels in information gathering and decision making as appropriate.	1 2 3 4 5
7. Organization—I determine the assignments of myself and other personnel.	1 2 3 4 5
8. Resource management—I allocate time and resources so that projects are completed within budget.	1 2 3 4 5
9. Teamwork—I coordinate the activities of my staff with those of others to achieve interrelated goals.	1 2 3 4 5
10. Staff development—I motivate others and encourage them to develop their skills and capabilities.	1 2 3 4 5

Scoring: Add the numbers circled for each item, and multiply the total by two. A perfect score is 100. You can consider your evaluation on the scale *excellent* if you scored between 90 and 100. Your score is *very good* if it is between 80 and 89. Between 70 and 79, consider your work *satisfactory*. If your score is between 60 and 69, it is *minimally satisfactory*. Below 60, your work is *unsatisfactory* or *poor*.

Total Score _____

Summary Worksheet

In this chapter, you saw the methods that employers use to evaluate employees and the relationship between evaluation and raises. You also saw that there were more similarities than differences across industries and in various sizes of companies. You also had a chance to examine some of the evaluation procedures of your own organization. Finally, you had a chance to evaluate your own work. Use the worksheet below to summarize and total your ratings.

Regardless of your job, you should have completed worksheets 1 and 2. In addition, if you have managerial responsibility, you will have completed worksheet 3. Copy your scores to the appropriate spaces below. Now total your scores. If you completed two worksheets, divide by two. If you completed three worksheets, divide by three. You now have the grand total of your job performance self-evaluation.

Rating on Worksheet 1—Overall Job Performance   _____

Rating on Worksheet 2—Specific Job Performance   _____

Rating on Worksheet 3—Managerial Performance   _____

   Add 1 and 2 or 1, 2, and 3   _____

   Divide by 2 (if you completed two worksheets)   _____

    or by 3 (if you completed three worksheets)   _____

Grand Total of Job Performance Self-evaluation   _____

A perfect score is 100. You can consider your evaluation on the scale *excellent* if you scored between 90 and 100. Your score is *very good* if it is between 80 and 89. Between 70 and 79, consider your work *satisfactory*. If your score is between 60 and 69, it is *minimally satisfactory*. Below 60, your work is *unsatisfactory* or *poor.*

Note: It is highly unlikely that you are perfect. Few of us are. If you achieved a perfect score, it would be a good idea to review your responses to see where you may have overrated your performance.

Sometimes I'm Happy . . .

In the previous chapter, you looked at your performance on the job from your employer's or supervisor's point of view. You evaluated how you were doing on the job using the frame of reference that your employer uses. This chapter changes the point of view. Instead of pointing the evaluation camera at your work, you will point it at the job itself. The purpose of this chapter is to help you find out how satisfied you are with the job you currently hold—both in terms of the occupation you are in and in terms of the organization for which you work.

Suppose you were asked the question, "How do you like your work?" What would be your response? Listen to the following sample answers for the kinds of things people talk about.

> I like the work of my job. I really like finding solutions to the problems and getting the people in

my group to carry them out. But I just can't stand the guy I work under. He's just sitting it out, waiting to retire. His idea of a good day is when *nothing* happens.

This started out as a great job, lots of opportunities to move ahead and make real money. Then the recession seemed to hit us and stay with us. I'm lucky if I just keep the customers I have, let alone finding new ones.

When you work for a big company like I do, it's sometimes hard to see where your work fits in to the whole thing. On the other hand, you know exactly how you are supposed to carry out your job because it's all spelled out, and you know this company has been around forever, and as long as I do my job right—and I *always* do it right—I will have a job and a decent salary.

There are five different aspects of job satisfaction mentioned in the sample answers. The first answer mentioned achievement, relationships with co-workers, and supervision. In the second answer, advancement and salary were the key factors, and in the third answer, security was most important. Each of us values different aspects of work, and how satisfying or dissatisfying your current job is for you is related both to what is important to you and to the reality of the job situation.

There has been a great deal of research on the factors that people generally find significant in job satisfaction. In the first part of this chapter, you will see the most important factors and be able to rate your job on them. In the second part of the chapter, you will be able to figure out which of the factors are most important to you and reach some conclusions about what it is you want in a job. By the end of the third section, you will have figured out whether the next move you want to make is further up in the organization for which you currently work, across to another job in a different organization, or out of this occupation. All of these are ways to make the right career moves.

How Satisfying Is My Current Job?

If you have the feeling that you really like your work most of the time—that you are eager to get to the office, the store, the factory, or the showroom to get on with what you left behind yesterday—you are motivated. On the other hand, if you have the feeling that you would rather pull the covers over your head and stay in bed—you just want to stay put—you are unmotivated. Of course most people have some mixture of these feelings. Examining the factors related to job satisfaction and motivation will help you see where the balance is for you at this time.

A number of researchers have studied what makes some people more satisfied on their jobs than others. These researchers have developed categories of job factors that are closely associated with the motivation to work harder. Employers are concerned with worker motivation because unmotivated workers produce less. However, our individual motivation is important to each of us. The word *motivation* comes from the same root as the word *move.* By looking at the factors related to job satisfaction, you can see how moved toward or away from your current job you are.

Factors related to job satisfaction and motivation are identified in two of the most important books in this area, *The Motivation to Work* by Frederick Herzberg, Bernard Mausner, and Barbara Snyderman and *Work and Motivation* by Victor Vroom. Twenty factors drawn from these books, along with an explanation of how to interpret each of them, are given in the list that follows. After the list, there is a worksheet to help you rate your current job in terms of these factors.

Twenty factors related to job satisfaction

1. Recognition—Acts or statements that show your supervisor knows how good or bad your work is.

2. Achievement—Seeing the results of your work in such ways as the completion of a project or finding the solution to a problem.

3. Possibility of growth—How you judge your opportunities to rise in the organization.

4. Advancement—Actual changes in your status in the organization.

5. Salary—Your current compensation and increases you have received.

6. Interpersonal relations—How you get along in the working situation with your associates and people who work under you.

7. Technical supervision—The knowledge and ability of your supervisor to judge your work fairly and to help you do it better.

8. Supervisory consideration—The extent to which you feel your supervisor thinks of you as a human being rather than just someone to get the work done.

9. Influence on decision making—The opportunities you have to participate in making decisions that affect your work.

10. Responsibility—How much authority you have over your own work and the work of others.

11. Company policy and administration—How well you feel the organization does as a whole in setting policies for personnel and carrying them out.

12. Working conditions—How you feel about physical conditions such as lighting and ventilation and getting equipment you need.

13. Hours of work—How comfortable you feel with the usual schedule of work and any need for work outside the regular schedule such as overtime, evening, or weekend work.

14. Effect on personal life—How the job affects you through travel, transfer policy, and other matters that directly affect your life outside of work.

15. Status—Any aspects of your job such as having a private secretary, a corner office, or the key to the executive restroom, which set you above or below others in the organization.

16. Job security—Company policy on tenure and the stability or instability of the company itself.

17. Work of the job—How you feel about the tasks or responsibilities you carry out.

18. Interest of the job—How bored or stimulated you feel during the actual carrying out of your job duties.

19. Control of work methods—How much freedom you have to carry out your job in the way you feel works best.

20. Use of skills and abilities—How much of your talents, knowledge, skills, and abilities are used in carrying out your work.

Rating Worksheet—Job Satisfaction

Directions: Now that you have looked over the twenty key factors related to job satisfaction, use them to rate your current job. Use the same rating scale you used to rate your job performance in the previous chapter.

1 = poor or well below average
2 = fair or below average
3 = satisfactory or average
4 = good or above average
5 = excellent or outstanding

If any of the items on the scale seem unclear, go back to the definitions for further explanation.

Factors	Rating				
1. Recognition—My supervisor knows how good my work is.	1	2	3	4	5
2. Achievement—I often enjoy seeing the results of my work.	1	2	3	4	5
3. Possibility of growth—I have good opportunities to rise in this organization.	1	2	3	4	5
4. Advancement—I have already improved my position in the organization.	1	2	3	4	5
5. Salary—My current compensation is fair for the job I am now doing.	1	2	3	4	5
6. Interpersonal relations—I get along in the working situation with my associates and people who work under me.	1	2	3	4	5
7. Technical supervision—My supervisor judges my work fairly and helps me do it better.	1	2	3	4	5
8. Supervisory consideration—My supervisor thinks of me as a human being rather than just someone to get the work done.	1	2	3	4	5
9. Influence on decision making—I participate in making decisions that affect my work.	1	2	3	4	5
10. Responsibility—I have authority over my own work and the work of others, if any report to me.	1	2	3	4	5
11. Company policy—The organization's personnel policies benefit me.	1	2	3	4	5
12. Working conditions—The physical conditions of work are comfortable.	1	2	3	4	5
13. Hours of work—The working hours are the ones I like.	1	2	3	4	5
14. Effect on personal life—The job suits the way I like to live.	1	2	3	4	5
15. Status—I have the office or company privileges that I should have.	1	2	3	4	5
16. Job security—This job will probably be mine for as long as I want it.	1	2	3	4	5

17. Work of the job—I am doing work that I enjoy and consider important to me.		1	2	3	4	5
18. Interest of the job—I often feel interested in what I am doing on a day-to-day basis.		1	2	3	4	5
19. Control of work methods—I choose how I want to do a job because I know how it should be done.		1	2	3	4	5
20. Use of skills and abilities—This job taps the things I know how to do best.		1	2	3	4	5

Scoring: Add the numbers circled for each item. A perfect score is 100. You can consider your evaluation on the scale *excellent* if you scored between 90 and 100. Your score is *very good* if it is between 80 and 89. Between 70 and 79, consider your work *satisfactory*. If your score is between 60 and 69, it is *minimally satisfactory*. Below 60, your work is *unsatisfactory* or *poor*.

_____
Total Score

What Is Most Important to Me?

When you completed the job rating sheet, you gave all twenty factors equal weight. However, different people place different values on each of the factors. They are probably not all equally important to you. Remember the examples at the beginning of the chapter? Some people would rank achievement as the most important factor in job satisfaction, others would choose job security, and still others salary. In fact, each of the factors probably has been chosen as most important by someone. This section of the chapter is designed to help you figure out what is most important to you as you progress toward deciding how to move ahead.

Worksheet—Weighing the Job Satisfaction Factors

Directions: Here is a worksheet to help you look at the job satisfaction factors in a different way. You are going to reorder the list so that you can give weight to the factors you find most important. Look over the list. Put the five factors that are more important to you on the first five lines of the worksheet, the lines labeled "most important." Put the five factors that are somewhat important to you on the next five lines, the lines labeled "somewhat important." Then put the remaining ten factors on the lines labeled "less important." Finally, copy your rating for each factor from the job satisfaction worksheet. Remember that you can go back to the previous chapter to see the definitions of the factors or the statements about them in the worksheet.

The Factors:

Recognition

Achievement

Possibility of growth

Advancement salary

Interpersonal relations

Technical supervision

Supervisory consideration

Influence on decision making

Responsibility

Company policy

Working conditions

Hours of work

Effect on personal life

Status

Job security

Work of the job

Interest of the job

Control of work methods

Use of skills and abilities

Most Important (List the five factors of greatest importance to you; then copy their rating from the previous worksheet.)

Factors	Rating
_____	_____
_____	_____
_____	_____
_____	_____
_____	_____

Somewhat Important (List the five factors of next importance to you; then copy their ratings from the previous worksheet.)

Factors	Rating
_____	_____
_____	_____
_____	_____
_____	_____
_____	_____

Less Important (List the remaining ten factors; then copy their ratings from the previous worksheet.)

Factors	Rating
_____	_____
_____	_____
_____	_____
_____	_____
_____	_____
_____	_____
_____	_____
_____	_____

Scoring: You probably have an idea of how the scoring of your current job has already changed, if it has, just from looking at the levels of importance you assigned to each job satisfaction factor. However, you can also rescore your job satisfaction in five easy steps:

1. Add the ratings of the five *most important factors* and
    multiply the sum by 4.   Sum of first five _____ × 4 = _____

2. Add the ratings of the five *somewhat important factors* and
    multiply the sum by 2.   Sum of second five _____ × 2 = _____

3. Add the ratings of the ten *less important factors*.   Sum of final ten _____

4. Add the results of Steps 1, 2, and 3.   Total of 1, 2, and 3 _____

5. Divide the total by 2.   **Final Score** _____

Again, a perfect score is 100. You can consider your evaluation on the scale *excellent* if you scored between 90 and 100. Your score is *very good* if it is between 80 and 89. Between 70 and 79 consider your work *satisfactory*. If your score is between 60 and 69, it is minimally satisfactory. Below 60, your work is *unsatisfactory* or *poor*.

Another way to look at your level of satisfaction with your current job is to compare what you have with what you want. The same twenty job satisfaction factors can be expanded into your personal goal list so that you move toward choosing a job that provides the greatest satisfaction.

As you look at the job factors, try to be clear and concrete in your thinking. You might want to try to visualize yourself on your ideal job to get a picture of what you want.

Visualizing job satisfaction

To visualize your job satisfaction, sit in a comfortable place where you will not be disturbed for at least thirty minutes. Close your eyes. Breathe evenly and deeply, counting backwards slowly from ten. You might want to begin by picturing yourself waking up in the morning. How do you feel? Where are you? Picture the time you get to work. Look at the workplace. Imagine yourself actually performing on the job, interacting with fellow workers, with your boss. If you have any current job-related problems, such as finding day care for your child, try to envision how these problems are solved.

You will probably not be able to see all that you want to see the first time you try the visualization exercise. In fact, it is really desirable that you do it several times. Sometimes you can go into the exercise with a general feeling of questioning. Other times you may want to use one or more of the job satisfaction factors, particularly those that were most important to you.

You can do several things with the material that comes out of the visualization. You can use a small notebook to keep track of your desires. You can use the worksheet that follows to capture the information on what you want, or you can just keep it in your head. Remember, one of the most important aspects of career decision making is figuring out how to achieve your desires. The first step, identifying what you want, is crucial.

In the next worksheet, the job satisfaction factors are listed with spaces for you to write in the specific items that would bring you satisfaction. You can use these specifics to help you identify the particular ways in which your current job is or is not satisfying and to give direction to your career move. Be sure to pay particular attention to those factors that you ranked most important and somewhat important. If any of the job satisfaction factors are not meaningful, just skip them. By listing both what you desire and the current conditions, you will probably be able to identify those factors that you want to change and others that are satisfying to you and that you would like to retain in a new job.

Worksheet—Job Satisfaction Specifics

Directions: For each factor, first list the specifics you desire, then the conditions on your current job.

Sample: **Interpersonal Relations**
My desire: Working with people who are also interested in how our products affect the environment.
Current conditions: No one seems interested in anything but today's production figures or the latest football scores.

Recognition

My desire: _____

_____

_____

_____

_____

Current conditions: _____

_____

_____

_____

_____

Achievement

My desire: _____

_____

_____

_____

_____

Current conditions: _____

_____

_____

_____

_____

Possibility of Growth

My desire: _____

_____

_____

_____

_____

Current conditions: _____

_____

_____

_____

_____

Advancement

My desire: _____

_____

_____

_____

_____

Current conditions: _____

_____

_____

_____

_____

Salary

My desire: _____

_____

_____

Current conditions: _____

_____

_____

Interpersonal Relations

My desire: _____

_____

_____

_____

_____

Current conditions: _____

_____

_____

_____

_____

Technical Supervision

My desire: _____

_____

_____

_____

_____

Current conditions: _____

_____

_____

_____

_____

Supervisory Consideration

My desire: _____

_____

_____

_____

_____

Current conditions: _____

_____

_____

_____

_____

Influence on Decision Making

My desire: _____

_____

_____

_____

_____

Current conditions: _____

_____

_____

_____

_____

Responsibility

My desire: _____

_____

_____

_____

_____

Current conditions: _____

_____

_____

_____

_____

_____

Company Policy

My desire: _____

_____

_____

_____

_____

Current conditions: _____

_____

_____

_____

_____

Working Conditions

My desire: _____

_____

_____

_____

Current conditions: _____

_____

_____

_____

_____

_____

Hours of Work

My desire: _____

_____

_____

_____

_____

Current conditions: _____

_____

_____

_____

_____

Effect on Personal Life

My desire: _____

_____

_____

_____

_____

Current conditions: _____

_____

_____

_____

_____

Status

My desire: _____

_____

_____

_____

_____

Current conditions: _____

_____

_____

_____

_____

Job Security

My desire: _____

_____

_____

_____

_____

Current conditions: _____

_____

_____

_____

_____

Work of the Job

My desire: _____

_____

_____

_____

_____

_____

Current conditions: _____

_____

_____

_____

_____

Interest of the Job

My desire: _____

_____

_____

_____

_____

Current conditions: _____

_____

_____

_____

_____

Control of Work Methods

My desire: _____

_____

_____

_____

_____

Current conditions: _____

_____

_____

_____

_____

Use of Skills and Abilities

My desire: _____

_____

_____

_____

_____

Current conditions: _____

_____

_____

_____

_____

Next Move—Up, Across,
or Out?

You have been looking at the factors related to your job that bring you satisfaction and those that don't. It is now time to take a look at that job and separate your occupation from your organization. If you are dissatisfied with your work as well as the organization for which you work, it may be because neither of these is the right place for you any longer.

As we go through life, our orientation to the world and what we seek from it often changes. Many authors have studied and written about this subject. Carl Jung, in *Modern Man in Search of a Soul,* described the different stages of life and how our goals differ as we move from stage to stage. According to Jung, the first half of life is devoted to the "development of the individual, our entrenchment in the outer world, the propagation of our kind and the care of our children." In the second part of life, he suggested that it is important that we pay attention to our inner lives and culture. Middle-aged women's power to change careers, indeed to accomplish whatever they wish, is the subject of two books by Carolyn Heilbrun. One is a mystery novel written under the pen name of Amanda Cross entitled *Sweet Death, Kind Death;* the other is her study of women's biographies, *Writing a Woman's Life.* Erik Erikson divides life into stages. In the adult stages, we are concerned first with people, then with production of ideas or things, and finally with integration, in which we seek some order and meaning of our own lives within a larger order.

You may be reading this book because you want to continue in the direction you have started but be more successful or because you want to change direction. While changes in direction are often associated with being in midcareer or the famous midlife crisis, you need to consider what is right for you and what you seek from your career at this time.

One way you can consider what you seek from your career at this point in your life is to look back on the sources of job satisfaction you identified in the previous sections of this chapter. Consider your needs, interests, and abilities, and examine where you want to go next. The next step could be to move up in your current organization either by getting a raise in your present job or by changing jobs, to move across to another organization that will offer you more of what you want, or to move to a different occupation. The chapters of section II of this book will help you put your choice into action. However, at this time you may want to consider that choice.

If we look again at the job satisfaction factors, we can see that some of these are related more to the occupation and some to the organization in which you work. Others can be related to both. For example, how interesting your work is seems more directly related to your occupation since people in the same occupation tend to do the same things even though they work in different settings. However, your judgments about company policy are probably more related to the organization in which you work since the policies affect people in many occupations within that organization, particularly in larger companies. Your sense of achievement is a factor that could be affected by either your job or organization. If you are a teacher, for example, your achievement is directly tied to your work in the classroom with students and is less affected by the school you work in than by the job itself. On the other hand, if you are an office administrator, your sense of achievement may be affected by your assignments, and the company may be more involved in determining those. One more look at the job satisfaction factors will help clarify the relative satisfaction you are getting from your occupation and the organization that employs you. This time, you will identify which factors are related to occupational satisfaction versus those that are related to organizational satisfaction or dissatisfaction. There will be no numeric score at the end since we know some factors are more important to you than others, just a chance to look at the picture to help you make the right career moves.

Worksheet—Occupational versus Organizational Sources of Satisfaction

Directions: Decide whether each of the following job satisfaction factors is more related to your occupation or to the organization in which you work. Then decide whether it is currently a source of satisfaction, a plus, or a source of dissatisfaction, a minus. Place the plus or minus in the appropriate column.

Sample: Because you decided working conditions were not satisfying, you gave it a minus (–). Because working conditions were determined by the organization, which had its offices in an old building that was hot in summer and cold in winter, you put that minus in the column marked "organizationally related."

Job Satisfaction Factors	Occupationally Related	Organizationally Related
Recognition	_____	_____
Achievement	_____	_____
Possibility of growth	_____	_____
Advancement	_____	_____
Salary	_____	_____
Interpersonal relations	_____	_____
Technical supervision	_____	_____
Supervisory consideration	_____	_____
Influence on decision making	_____	_____
Responsibility	_____	_____
Company policy	_____	_____
Working conditions	_____	_____
Hours of work	_____	_____
Effect on personal life	_____	_____
Status	_____	_____
Job security	_____	_____
Work of the job	_____	_____
Interest of the job	_____	_____
Control of work methods	_____	_____
Use of skills and abilities	_____	_____

Summary Worksheet

In this chapter, you looked at some factors commonly associated with job satisfaction and evaluated your job on the basis of these factors. Then you ranked the job satisfaction factors to see which were more important to you and how that affected your feelings about your current job. You then went more deeply into your examination of the factors and identified the specific desires you have in relation to each factor. Finally, you thought about the relative importance to you of your current occupation and of your current organization. Here are four questions to sum up what you have been exploring in this chapter. The next to last question is the same as the one asked at the beginning of this chapter.

1. How involved do I feel in my current occupation?

_____

_____

_____

_____

_____

2. How committed do I feel to the organization for which I am now working?

_____

_____

_____

_____

_____

3. How do I like my work?

_____

_____

_____

_____

_____

4. What is the next career move for me?

_____

_____

_____

_____

_____

WHERE I WILL BE TOMORROW

Section II

Moving Ahead Right Here

After completing the worksheets in the last chapter and thinking about your career, you may feel that you are working for an organization that is pretty good for you, and you may have discovered that you like your job as well. Of course that does not mean that you want to stand still. You may want a higher salary or compensation package, greater recognition or independence on the job, or a better job within the organization.

This chapter provides you with strategies for getting raises and promotions, for moving up within the organization in which you now work. Because moving up is generally based on job performance, the chapter begins with a section on setting some self-improvement goals. Starting with the same performance evaluation sheets you used in chapter 1 and moving to an examination of other skills expected of those on the way up, you will be able to draft your own self-improvement goal sheet. In the second section of this chapter, you will hear from managers about effective ways of seeking a raise. The final section of the chapter will deal with promotions and job moves within your organization.

Setting Goals for Self-Improvement on the Job

All of the managers we spoke with stressed the importance of job performance in two areas. One area is called *production skills* and the other area is called *process skills*.

Production skills

Production skills are specific to each occupation and are typically more easily measured by some form of end product or output. For example, measures of production skills might include how many dollars in sales you brought in during a particular quarter, or whether the program you were assigned to write was completed on time, or how many billable client hours you brought into your law firm. Production skills also include the knowledge and techniques you need to accomplish the job. For example, in sales, production skills include your ability to use leads, your development of sales plans for clients, and your knowledge of closing strategies. As another example, in teaching, your production skills include knowledge of the subject matter, ability to construct a lesson plan, and awareness of the different learning styles of students.

Process skills

Process skills, on the other hand, cut across occupations and industries and are more difficult to measure than production skills. Measurement of process skills is more an estimate of how you got to the end product than what that end product was. Although process skills may seem intangible and difficult to measure, they are often the key to success on the job. Examples of process skills include all areas related to communications and interpersonal relations. One of the employers we interviewed said the worst thing an employee can do is "be stupid." For a moment, we might think that the employer was referring to production skills, that the employee did not know how to do her or his job. But here is the rest of what the employer said, "I can't stand it when people have a blank look. I'm telling them how to do something, and they're standing there with a blank look and a head bobbing up and down like one of those dolls people put in the back of their cars. They hope that when they leave, understanding will come to them like a bolt of lightning. If they were not stupid, they would ask for further instructions and let me go over it again." That employer has given a good description of how he observes the process skill of listening.

Let's take another look at the first rating worksheet you completed in chapter 1. There are twenty items on the list, which was compiled from several organizations. Only the first five deal with production skills. The remaining fifteen are process skills.

Frequently rated production skills

1. Job understanding—I understand clearly the responsibilities and tasks of my job.

2. Job knowledge—I know how to do my job well.

3. Quality of work—I am proud of the work I produce.

4. Quantity of work—I produce as much or more work as others in my job or department.

5. Expense control—I operate within the time, money, or other resources allotted.

Frequently rated process skills

6. Listening skill—I can follow instructions or information delivered orally from others.

7. Oral communication skill—I feel comfortable expressing my ideas in planned or informal meetings.

8. Written communication skill—My memos and letters to others are clear and complete.

9. General communication—I share information with my subordinates, superiors, and fellow workers.

10. Responsibility—I complete assignments in the time specified.

11. Cooperation—I work well with associates, subordinates, supervisors, and others to achieve common goals.

12. Creativity—I find new ways to get things done better and communicate them to others.

13. Initiative—I work on my own to get things done.

14. Judgment—I make decisions that work out well for the department or company.

15. Adaptability—I can adjust to new situations.

16. Independence—I can work with little or no supervision.

17. Reliability—I follow work instructions and company policy.

18. Motivation—I show interest in and enthusiasm for my work.

19. Attitude—I accept criticism and see it as a way to improve my work.

20. Leadership—I can often persuade others to do things a better way.

Three goal-setting worksheets follow. They all begin with the self-evaluation you carried out when you read chapter 1. (If you did not start with chapter 1, you might want to go back to it now.) The first goal-setting worksheet helps you identify areas for self-improvement in the twenty production and process skills just discussed. The second helps you focus on your specific job responsibilities, and the third is for you if you have or want to have a managerial position.

Goal setting   Goal setting is an exercise in which you identify behaviors you want to improve and decide upon a way to do it. The more specific you can be, the more helpful the material will be to you when you re-read it. As an example, let's return to that employee with poor listening skills, the one whose head just kept bobbing up and down. Suppose this person were aware that her or his supervisor thought listening skills should be improved. In the space next to "listening," he or she might write the following goal statement: "Whenever I get instructions, I will be sure I know what to do before I begin doing it. The next three times I am given oral instructions, I will ask at least one question before I leave the room."

If your organization has an employee rating form that is given to you, you may also want to develop some self-improvement goals based on your most recent ratings. Often we tend to dismiss ratings that are different from those we would give ourselves. Try to be open to what your supervisor has said about you through these ratings. Of course your supervisor does not know you as well as you know yourself, and the supervisor has her or his own opinions and biases. However, the rating does reflect how you appear to at least one person who is important in determining your access to career moves within the organization.

If you have a good relationship with your supervisor or a co-worker, you might want to involve that person in your goal setting. However, you should not turn to someone else to set the goals for you. Once you have reflected upon them and narrowed them down, you may just want to check them out.

At this point, do not worry about how many goals you are setting or how you will accomplish them all. What you are trying to do now is look at all the opportunities you have for the right career moves at your current job. At the end of this section, you will have the opportunity to zero in on the most important steps to take next.

Goal-Setting Worksheet 1—Production and Process Skills

Directions: Knowing the importance of both production and process skills can now help you begin to set specific goals for self-improvement. Again, use the items from the first rating worksheet. Look back to chapter 1 and copy the rating you gave yourself for each item there onto this worksheet. Then circle the items where you would like to improve your performance. For each item circled, write a goal that will help you improve your performance in that area of production or process skills.

Rating	Item	Goal
_____	1. Job understanding	_____ _____ _____
_____	2. Job knowledge	_____ _____ _____
_____	3. Quality of work	_____ _____ _____
_____	4. Quantity of work	_____ _____ _____
_____	5. Expense control	_____ _____ _____
_____	6. Listening skill	_____ _____ _____

_____ 7.   Oral communication skill   _____

                                                    _____

                                                    _____

_____ 8.   Written communication skill   _____

                                                    _____

                                                    _____

_____ 9.   General communication   _____

                                                    _____

                                                    _____

_____ 10.   Responsibility   _____

                                                    _____

                                                    _____

_____ 11.   Cooperation   _____

                                                    _____

                                                    _____

_____ 12.   Creativity   _____

                                                    _____

                                                    _____

_____ 13.   Initiative   _____

                                                    _____

                                                    _____

_____ 14.   Judgment   _____

                                                    _____

                                                    _____

_____ 15.   Adaptability   _____

                                                    _____

                                                    _____

_____ 16.   Independence   _____

                                                    _____

                                                    _____

_____ 17.   Reliability   _____

                                                    _____

                                                    _____

_____ 18.   Motivation   _____

                                                    _____

                                                    _____

_____ 19.   Attitude   _____

                                                    _____

                                                    _____

_____ 20.   Leadership   _____

                                                    _____

                                                    _____

Goal-Setting Worksheet 2—Specific Job Responsibilities

Directions: Remember that in chapter 1 you also identified the five most important responsibilities of your job. This is a way of zeroing in on the key production skills required of you. To complete this worksheet, you will need to turn back to chapter 1. Copy a few key words from the five job responsibilities you identified in chapter 1. Copy your rating as well, and circle the responsibilities where you can see room for self-improvement. For each circled responsibility, write a goal statement.

Rating   **Item**

_____ Job responsibility 1   _____

Goal _____

_____

_____ Job responsibility 2   _____

Goal _____

_____

_____ Job responsibility 3   _____

Goal _____

_____

_____ Job responsibility 4   _____

Goal _____

_____

_____ Job responsibility 5   _____

Goal _____

_____

Goal-Setting Worksheet 3—Managerial Responsibilities

Directions: If you are in a managerial position or hope to be in one, there is one last rating sheet to review in chapter 1, "Rating Worksheet 3—Managerial Performance." Look back to chapter 1 and copy the rating you gave yourself for each item there onto this worksheet. Then circle the items where you would like to improve your performance. For each item circled, write a goal that will help you improve your performance in that area of managerial responsibilities. If any of the items are not clear, remember to look at their definitions given in chapter 1.

Rating		Item	Goal
_____	1.	Leadership	_____
			_____
			_____
			_____
_____	2.	Problem analysis	_____
			_____
			_____
			_____
_____	3.	Problem solution	_____
			_____
			_____
			_____
_____	4.	Planning	_____
			_____
			_____
			_____
_____	5.	Flexibility	_____
			_____
			_____

_____   6.   Delegation _____

_____

_____

_____

_____   7.   Organization _____

_____

_____

_____

_____   8.   Resource management _____

_____

_____

_____

_____   9.   Teamwork _____

_____

_____

_____

_____   10.   Staff development _____

_____

_____

_____

Get ready for tomorrow. Making the career moves on your job means not only improving what you are doing today but preparing for tomorrow. There are a number of ways you can do this, and one of the most important is to stay abreast of current information. The period in which we are living is sometimes called the information age. It is certainly true that the person who has information is ahead of those who don't.

Use the resources for information that are available to you. Read the daily newspaper. Know what is going on in the town or city in which you work as well as in the industry in which you are employed. This may mean reading not only a local paper but a business paper such as the *Wall Street Journal* or the business section of the *New York Times*. The science, health, education, and general news sections of the *Times* and other major papers also often provide valuable information you can use on your job. Magazines like *Business Week* also can give you valuable insights. Remember, there is no such animal as information presented without a point of view. The more sources you read, the more complete the picture you will get.

If there is a professional organization in your field, you should also consider joining it or subscribing to its publications. Of course the important thing here is to read the publications, not just receive them.

Electronic data bases and bulletin boards are growing in popularity. If you have access to one or more of these, you have another useful resource.

Know what is happening in your organization. Does your organization publish a company newsletter or magazine? While a lot of the material in house organs is social, there may also be nuggets about directions the company is taking that will prove useful to you in moving ahead. Is there a stockholders' or annual report? Again, you may be able to see areas of company expansion that will have career meaning for you.

Finally, be prepared for the crises and changes that can spell opportunity for you. Try to imagine what it would be like if you suddenly had to take on your boss's job. Think about the greatest problem facing your company or the unit of your company in which you work. If you had the power, how would you solve that problem? What is the worst thing that could go wrong in your organization or unit? What could you do in that kind of pinch that would help the situation?

Goal-Setting Worksheet 4—Getting Ready for Tomorrow

Directions: Use this worksheet to identify one goal that will help you increase your knowledge base about work and one goal that will help you be prepared for an opportunity within your organization or unit.

Goal 1. I will increase my knowledge base by _____

_____

_____

_____

_____

_____

_____

Goal 2. I am preparing for the challenge of change and the opportunity of crises by thinking about

what I would do if _____

_____

_____

_____

_____

_____

_____

Summary Goal-Setting Worksheet

Directions: It is time to review the goals you have written and choose those that are most important to you now. When any of us try to make too many changes at once, we often give up in frustration. Look over all the goals you have listed. Select no more than five. List them below. Then number them in order of importance to you. Finally, put a starting date next to each goal. It is a good idea not to start working on all of them at once. Try to leave at least two weeks between start-up dates.

Goal	Rank	Start Date
_____	____	_____
_____		
_____	____	_____
_____		
_____	____	_____
_____		
_____	____	_____
_____		
_____	____	_____
_____		

Seeking and Getting a Raise

As we have seen, most organizations have some formal system for evaluating salaries and granting raises. How well the system works varies from one organization to another. Therefore, you may find variations in how closely your raise is linked to your performance evaluation. The beginning of the chapter dealt with ways to improve your performance and, in this way, your performance rating. There are other techniques for successfully negotiating a salary increase, and the rest of this section of the chapter will deal with those.

Here are four rules for seeking and getting a raise given by managers responsible for granting those raises.

Four rules for getting the raise you want

1. Watch your timing.

2. Concentrate on accomplishments.

3. Know your dollar value in the marketplace.

4. Be aware of company pay scales.

Watch your timing

Watching your timing may be as important in seeking a salary raise as it is in comedy. In this case, however, you don't want to be laughed at. Timing is related to the schedule of reviews. It is not appropriate, for example, to seek a raise before the first review is scheduled or before you have worked for an organization for a year, unless there are truly exceptional circumstances.

One of the employers interviewed suggested that a good strategy is to find an opportunity to discuss your productivity with your supervisor when you know a review is about to take place. During that meeting, you might say something like, "I'd really like to end up with x dollars (filling in the x with a number, of course) when it's over." Another manager suggested waiting until the review is completed and then either accepting the raise offered or asking for more at that time. Part of that decision must be based on what is customary in your organization. Each organization has a culture of its own, and as in any culture, the unwritten rules are as important as those that have been formalized. There are several times that it is definitely not a good idea to ask for a raise. One of these is when you know your work is not being viewed as satisfactory. As one employer said, "Never ask for a raise on the heels of a reprimand." Another said, "If I've been yelling and screaming, it means I hope the person will quit. That is no time to ask me for a raise." Another example of poor timing is at a point just after raises have been negotiated or between evaluation cycles. All organizations run on budgets that are tied to various cycles of the business. Asking for a raise at the wrong point in the cycle seems to show that you are not "with it."

Concentrate on accomplishments

Concentrating on accomplishments is the most important thing you can do when you have decided that the time is right to negotiate a raise. Stress ways in which you have added to the company's productivity or income or helped reduce time or expenditures. Statements of accomplishments focus not only on what you have done but what you have contributed to the organization. Try to be as specific as possible. If you introduced a new traffic control system that has saved the company money in personnel time, estimate that time in annual dollar cost savings to present in your request. The idea is not necessarily to get a match dollar for dollar but to move the dialogue to a discussion of money issues.

Do not approach a discussion of salary with a focus on your needs. As one of our interviewed employers said, " 'The baby needs a new pair of shoes' just doesn't fit in the discussion of salaries. That may sound cold, but this business pays so much, and if it's not enough for you, you need to move to something else."

Know your dollar value in the marketplace

Knowing your dollar value in the marketplace of your job and your industry is essential in any negotiation. Are you an accountant with two years' experience? A computer programmer with knowledge of the most currently used programming languages? An office manager bilingual in Spanish? Although different occupations vary widely in the salaries and other compensations they offer, there are often similarities within an occupation. Differences in salary within an occupation are generally based on the person's number of years of experience and additional education or special licenses acquired, along with judgments about job performance. Sometimes additional variances are based on differences in the general cost of living from one area to another. Before you begin a salary negotiation, you need to get all the information you can on current salaries for your field of work.

There are a number of sources of salary information. Some professional associations regularly survey and publish salary information. The magazine *Working Woman* summarizes a number of these in an annual issue on salaries. Some state departments of labor collect salary data which is available in publications in your local library or by request to the appropriate state agency. Other information may be available from your regional office of the federal Bureau of Labor Statistics. Also, the Bureau of Labor Statistics publishes the *Occupational Outlook Handbook,* a biannual collection of information, including average salaries, for almost every occupation imaginable. In addition, some computer-based career information delivery systems have up-to-date, locally relevant wage data. As these systems become more widespread, you have a better chance of getting access to one of them through your local library or a community agency.

You should not use your knowledge of the prevailing wage for your job to threaten your boss with another job offer. You may be taken up on it.

Be aware of company pay scales

Being aware of company pay scales helps give you perspective on the more general wage information. If you have gotten one or more raises that were at the top of the general range of percentages or if you have reached the top of the scale for your position, you may find that an excellent performance rating will not yield as good a raise as those you have received in the past. This may be the time to think of promotion or other job satisfactions that are important to you.

You can use your knowledge of the company pay scale in a wage negotiation to point out inequities between your pay and that of your peers. Before you do this, however, it is important that you carefully compare the responsibilities, experience, education, and performance of those whose salary you are using as a basis for your request. You do not want to be denied a raise because you did not have the facts right.

The following worksheet will help you marshal your arguments and plan your strategy for negotiating the best possible raise.

Raise Request Worksheet

1. How has my work contributed to the product or service of the organization?

_____

_____

_____

_____

_____

2. What special projects or activities that contributed to the product or service of the organization have I been involved in?

_____

_____

_____

_____

_____

3. How have I helped the organization reduce the cost of doing business in the past year?

_____

_____

_____

_____

_____

4. What new responsibilities have I assumed in the last year?

_____

_____

_____

_____

5. What new skills have I acquired which I am now using on the job?

_____

_____

_____

_____

6. For persons of education and experience similar to mine, what is the average national or local salary?

_____

7. What is the salary range for my position in my organization?

From _____ to _____.

8. What factors determine where someone is on that range?

_____

_____

_____

_____

9. What is the best time in the business year to ask for a raise?

_____

_____

10. What salary will I ask for (or be satisfied with)?

_____

Getting Promoted   If you are at the point where you want to change jobs within the same organization, you need to take a look at the routes and methods that are in place. Changing jobs means either moving up for a promotion or across in a lateral move to a job that you would find more satisfying.

In a large or small organization, the opportunity to move may be presented to you by someone else. Many of us cherish the image of the ideal boss, an angel hovering over us who sees the brilliance of our work and the energy in our endeavors and who therefore taps us on the shoulder to say, "You are ready now. Come with me to the next rung of the ladder." While this sometimes happens, it is also often preferable to pave the way yourself by seeking and taking the opportunities for promotion or movement. Here are five tips for getting the job you want within your current organization.

Five tips for successful in-house job changes

1. Know the possible jobs in your organization and which one is right for you.

2. Know your organization's policies and procedures for job change.

3. Use the career development services of the organization.

4. Take advantage of educational opportunities.

5. Be on the lookout for the right moment to make your move.

Know about possible jobs   In a small, informal organization, you may create an opportunity by seeking out your supervisor and identifying the job you would like. Of course you must observe the realities of the organization. If there is no vice president, just the boss and the rest of the workers like you, it is unlikely that such a position will be created unless you can make a very good case for it. In fact, it is generally true that while there are more opportunities to have your work recognized in a small company, there may also be fewer places to which you can move.

Know policies and procedures   In a large organization, there is usually some mechanism for internal movement. To take advantage of an opening, you need to know your organization. Some companies have career ladders. A career ladder is a path that many people are expected to take with, however, fewer and fewer positions as the rungs get higher. An example of a career ladder could be moving from typist in the pool, to secretary, to a middle-management executive, to office manager. Another career ladder is from sales clerk, to department manager, to a position in the management of the company as a whole.

Use career development services

If you are working for a large company, the personnel department or human resources department may have someone similar to a career counselor who is there to help you make your next move within the organization. You can ask if your organization has such a person or department, or you can watch for evidence of it. Usually if there is an active personnel department, you will see notices of jobs on bulletin boards or in company newsletters.

Among the services that you might find in a company's career development program are individual counseling, career development seminars or courses, the opportunity to take interest inventories, help in decision-making skills, help with substance abuse problems, and management development programs. It is a rare company program that offers all of these services.

Take advantage of educational opportunities.

In addition to providing information on career opportunities, many companies will help you pay for additional education. Usually the courses you take or the degree you seek must be related to what you are doing and the work of the company. If you have not completed college, you may be able to do so with a major in accounting or marketing or some other area of study the company considers useful to it. If you have completed college, you may be able to take graduate-level courses. In some companies, the reimbursement is related to your grade in the course. An A will get you 100-percent reimbursement; a B, 75 percent; and so on. Again, you need to be observant and seek the information you want.

The need for continuing education and training, whether paid for by your company or you, cannot be stressed enough. In 1986, the National Alliance of Business assessed the changes taking place in our society today to make some predictions. The publication *Employment*

Policies: Looking to the Year 2000 states: "There will be fewer natural career ladders. The new technology makes it increasingly feasible to separate 'back office' functions (clerical, service workers) from 'front office' (technical, sales, professional, management). It will thus become more difficult to work up the ranks through informal on-the-job training. More formalized training may be necessary."

Know when to make your move

By examining the job postings within the organization as well as becoming familiar with the informal structure and how it works, you can set the stage for your promotion. A key element is the ability to take advantage of opportunities. One of the managers interviewed described an employee in a systems analysis group who seemed willing enough but was not performing as well as others. On a scale of 1 to 5, this person got mostly 3s. There were just too many errors in the employee's work. The employee took the opportunity to explain to the supervisor that he was on the wrong track. He had felt this for a while and thought he had been sending signals, but they were not clear enough. As a result of this conversation, the supervisor recommended the individual for another job. The employee transferred and has been earning 4+ ratings since then.

When you are first hired, you are selected on the basis of what people think you can do. When you are promoted, it is on the basis of what you have done. The formal or informal rating of your performance and the actions you take to improve your performance are often crucial. Thinking of promotion, therefore, brings us back to the beginning of this chapter and your analysis of how to improve on your job.

Of course you may find in your analysis that there is nowhere else you want to go in the organization for which you work but that you are ready for new challenges and opportunities. If so, the next chapters on finding a job, résumé writing, and interviewing will be of help to you.

In the worksheet that follows, there are some questions you can use to assess the opportunities for you in the company where you are now working.

Promotions Opportunity Worksheet

1. What help is provided in career development by the organization?

_____

_____

2. Is there a bulletin board or company newsletter that lists opportunities for promotion?

_____

3. What jobs in the company are of interest to me as my next move?

_____

_____

_____

6. For which of those opportunities am I qualified?

_____

_____

7. What can I do to improve my qualifications?

_____

_____

_____

8. What help can I get from the company with my education?

_____

_____

_____

9. What procedures do I follow to get the promotion I want?

_____

_____

_____

Summary Worksheet

In this chapter, you saw how employers are interested both in performance and attitudes, and you identified ways of improving your own work. With this background, you then examined winning strategies for negotiating a raise and for seeking and getting a promotion or move to a job you would find more desirable.

Use the following checklist to review the major ideas in this chapter.

_____ I understand the difference between production skills and process skills.

_____ I have identified at least one but no more than five goals for self-improvement on the job.

_____ I have set a date to begin work on each goal.

_____ I know where to get information about wages that I can use in salary negotiations.

_____ I have identified the ways in which I have helped the organization, and I can use these in discussing a raise.

_____ I am planning the best time to ask for a raise.

_____ I know the next job I want in this organization.

_____ I know the career development services offered by my organization.

_____ I know how to go about getting a promotion.

Moving Out—How to Find the Right Job 4

In the last three chapters, we looked at your career in your current job and then at moving ahead in your current company. This chapter takes us on a new path. It is about the career moves to make if you want to leave the organization you now work for. In the first section of this chapter, you will see the factors to consider when thinking about making a change. This section will help you answer the question "Should I move out?" The second section gives you some ideas for dealing with the question "Where do I want to go?" and suggests some sources of help in making the decision. The final section of this chapter has information on resources for finding the right job openings. It will help you answer the question "How do I get there from here?"

Should I Move Out?   Carrying out the self-examination and the analysis of your organization in the first three chapters may have led you to the idea that the next correct career move for you is out of the current job you hold and out of that organization. Five questions that you can now ask—and answer—will help you make the decision.

Five questions about moving out

1. Is my current occupation bringing me the satisfaction I want?
2. Do I get the support I think is important from the organization for which I work?
3. Is there room for my professional growth in this organization?
4. Is my work evaluated and rewarded appropriately in this organization?
5. Am I being sent signals that it is time to leave?

You have already answered the first two questions about occupational and organizational satisfaction when you completed chapter 2. If you are not satisfied with your current occupation, then you will want to change your field of work, and it is time to look for a new job. Similarly, if you are not getting the kind of support from your organization that you need, then it is time to find a new job in a different company or institution, although you may not want to change your field of work. If you answered no to either of the first two questions, it is time for you to move out.

You have also answered the next two questions, this time when you completed chapter 3. If you feel that your work is undervalued, you will want to change jobs to a company or institution where you will receive the compensation you think is right. Remember to be aware of going market wages for your occupation and level of experience. On the other hand, you may feel your work is correctly valued, but there is no place for you to move in your current organization. Sometimes there is no place to move up because the organization is too small to have the next position you could fill. Sometimes there is no place to move up because all of the positions immediately above yours are filled with people who do not seem ready to move on themselves. If you answered no to either the third or fourth questions, it is time for you to move out.

Signals from the organization that it is time for you to move out can take several forms. There may be a period of budgetary retrenchment in which you are offered a compensation package for leaving. You need to weigh what you will get against your needs and the possibility of getting the kind of job you want elsewhere. You may also have heard through the grapevine or by reading information sources such as business periodicals and annual reports that there is going to be a reduction in force. Do not let this panic you, but do use the news to get yourself in a position to move if you need and want to. Finally, you may be receiving personal signals that it is time to leave. One of the managers we interviewed said, "We don't practice an 'up and out' policy. If someone is content to continue at the same level, we generally let them stay. However, you can get the message if you are not getting raises and you are getting fewer work assignments than others at your level." If the answer to the fifth question is yes, you are getting signals to leave, and the right career move is out.

A few words of caution on the decision to move out. First, do not make the decision in a moment of anger or frustration. The truth is you will probably experience some anger or frustration wherever you work and whatever your job. Have a plan before you leave. Second, it is generally a good idea to do your job search while you have a job. Therefore, if you have a choice, do not leave your job until you have another, unless you are planning to return to school full-time or do something else worthwhile before looking for a new job. It gives employers more confidence to hire someone who is working. Third, do not telegraph your plans to leave by slacking off on work. This can only hurt you in the long run.

Have you ever heard people say "I wish they would fire me"? People who say this are not prepared to make the right career moves. Take charge of your own career. If it is indeed time to move out, begin to move. Do not wait for them to move you. Of course sometimes there is a sudden reduction in force, a takeover or merger, that leaves you without a job. If that is the case, avoid self-blame and move on to the next steps.

Four tips on moving out

1. Take charge of your own career.
2. Do not quit in a moment of anger.
3. Do not telegraph your plans to leave by doing less work.
4. If possible, conduct your job search while you have a job.

Where Do I Want to Go?

There are no rules on where you should go in your career. In fact, the very definition of career is unique to each individual. Your career is the path of education, work, and related experiences that you have taken. You have to decide whether this is the place on that path to move straight ahead, to turn, or to widen the path to look at other options.

Consider the future of the job market

Most projections of the coming job market agree on several important factors that you may want to take into consideration in deciding upon your next move. The first is that people will tend to change not only jobs but occupations several times in their lives. The second is that there will be less security within organizations, so cases of individuals who stay with the same company throughout their entire career will be less frequent. Third, technology will continue to change the nature of jobs themselves and the tasks performed on those jobs.

What do these projections mean to you? They mean that your desire to move out at this point in your career is probably a good one. They also mean that part of your plan for making the right career moves should include a plan for more education. This education can range from formal courses in a degree program at a university to teaching yourself the latest computer applications in your field.

These projections also mean that your search for a new job can be wider than it would have been ten years ago. Transferring the skills from an occupation in one industry to a similar occupation in a different industry is now more possible than it was in the past. Articles in the *New York Times* and the magazine *Working Woman* have pointed out some of the challenges you will encounter in switching industries. The challenges include identifying the organization you want to work for, learning the language of the new industry, and having a strong commitment to change.

Analyze job satisfaction factors

To identify the organization you want to work for, you need to make some decisions about the factors most important to you. You might want to look back at chapter 2 and your weighting of job satisfaction factors. You will be considering the kind of culture or feeling you want in the company. For example, do you like a large, highly structured organization, or do you prefer a company that feels like a family? Then you can identify companies in the geographic area in which you want to work. In the next step, you need to find people from your target companies to talk to. Perhaps you know people who work with or for the companies on your list. The people you know may lead you to others. Through these informational interviews, you will be able to get a feel for the organization that interests you. Finally, you will need to learn what opportunity in that company will fit your skills.

Learn the language of the industry

Learning the language of the new industry is critical to your convincing your potential new employers that they should take a chance on you. For example, if you have been a teacher, and now you want to work in corporate training programs, you need to learn to talk about "program design" rather than "curriculum development." The last section of this chapter will help you find other sources of help in changing industries, and the chapters on résumé writing and interview skills will have more on fitting your abilities to the employer's needs.

Be committed to change

A strong commitment to change is essential in this process because it is not easy. Although there are managers who are willing to take a chance on a good person who has a nontraditional background for a particular job, there are also others who are more set in their ways. People who have changed industries also find their job hunt is time consuming. It may take several months for you to find the right position in the right company. Finally, you may also need a commitment to reeducation so that you can learn the skills you need to augment the ones you already have.

Changing industries is similar to changing occupations. In both cases you take the skills and interests you have and move them to a situation that better suits your needs and desires. In fact, when you move from one industry to another, your occupation may be a different one. The teacher in a school becomes a trainer in the corporate world. However, you may be interested in making a more drastic occupation change. If you want to change occupations and you are uncertain of what you want to do next, you can get help from career counselors or work through the career decision-making process on your own.

Seek outside help   Career counselors can help you identify your interests, skills, values, and needs and relate those to occupations through a variety of services. They administer interest inventories and work with you to interpret the results. They provide information on occupations or lead you to sources of this information. They offer individual or group counseling to help you explore how all of it comes together for you, and they assist you in taking the next steps in the job search. Career counselors may be in private practice or work for counseling services or clinics. The National Career Development Association, a professional organization of counselors, has prepared consumer guidelines for selecting a career counselor. You will find these guidelines at the end of this book in appendix A.

Career counseling is also offered at some community agencies and universities. You can find out about these through local libraries, from your clergyperson, or by contacting a university directly. Some state employment services also offer testing. Sometimes this is available only to certain groups, such as those between the ages of sixteen and twenty-one or those who are starting to work after being homemakers. Your local telephone directory will lead you to your state employment service.

Some people prefer to work through the process of career decision making on their own. If you would like to do that, your local library is a valuable resource. The local public library or community college may provide access to a computer-based career information delivery system. These systems help you develop a list of careers that meet your interests, needs, and abilities. The systems then provide information on the careers, their entry-level requirements, the opportunities for advancement, and the industries in which they are most often found. Some systems will even provide information on specific employers in your state or region.

If you do not have access to a career information delivery system, your librarian can help you get more information about occupations that interest you. There are a number of books that can help you in this process. The *Occupational Outlook Handbook* provides excellent brief descriptions of jobs. If you want to read more about a particular occupation or industry, look for books like *Opportunities in High Tech Careers* or *Opportunities in Insurance Careers* in the VGM Career Horizons Opportunities series. There are truly hundreds of books about individual careers.

If you are changing occupations, taking a different turn in your career path, you may also want to contact the professional association related to your new occupation. A number of professional associations publish literature ranging from descriptions of the field to actual job search handbooks. For example, the Association for School, College and University Staffing (ASCUS) regularly publishes *A Job Search Handbook for Educators*. The ASCUS handbook not only gives valuable tips on conducting a job search in the field of education, it also provides a table of teacher supply and demand by region of the country and field of teaching. In addition, attending meetings of the local chapter of professional associations is an easy way of meeting people who can talk to you about the field. Some chapter meetings may provide formal programs that will also be of use. Finally, the people you meet may prove useful in the next step—getting the job.

Your search for new directions may take you in the direction of starting your own business. If you decide upon the entrepreneurial path, again, the library or bookstore will be of help. Look at the many self-help books available on the subject and select those that appear to be of greatest applicability to you. In New York City, the Executive Volunteer Corps offers free services to people interested in starting their own businesses. Additional help in starting your own business may be available from the federal Small Business Administration. Use the government information pages in your telephone directory to locate similar services where you live.

Checklist for Career Direction

Directions: To be sure you are using all the available resources in considering what your next career move should be, use the checklist below to review them. Place a check next to the ones that will be useful to you.

_____ 1. Reviewing my evaluation of the satisfactions and dissatisfactions with my job and my current organization (in chapter 2).

_____ 2. Examining the possibilities of transferring skills to another industry.

_____ 3. Talking to people I know who work with or for companies in other industries.

_____ 4. Setting up informational interviews with people who work for companies that interest me.

_____ 5. Using the services of a career counselor or service to help in the choice of a new occupation.

_____ 6. Using the services of the state employment service.

_____ 7. Using a computer-based career information delivery system.

_____ 8. Using print information on occupations in the library.

_____ 9. Getting printed information from a professional association.

_____ 10. Joining and attending meetings of a professional association.

How Do I Get There from Here?

There are four basic methods for seeking a job. There is no need for you to select only one method. A successful job campaign often includes the use of several or all of the methods. The four methods are:

1. Networking
2. Using professional employment services
3. Answering advertisements
4. Advertising yourself

Networking

Networking is a currently popular term that gives a technical sound to a method that people have been using for a very long time. Basically, it means that you tell all the people you know that you are looking for a job and ask them to help you. Do not think that you do not know anybody who can help you. Think of the word *network*. Picture a network. It is not a single string from you to one person and from you to another person. It is like a web with strings from you to the people you know and from them to the people they know. People generally like to help others. One reason is because it makes them feel good. The other is because it increases their own network of people they know.

The first thing to do is to make a list of everyone you know. Consider people from all aspects of your life: family; friends; parents or children of friends; teachers; fellow members of religious, professional, and community organizations; sports teammates or opponents; and people you work or do business with.

The next step is to think of what you want from each of these people. How can each one help you? Some may actually be employed by or run organizations in which you would like to work. Others may know people in the kind of organizations you would like to work for. Still others may be just a shot in the dark. That is, you can't think of how they can help you, but it is worth seeing if they can. Your approach to each person may have to be a little different. You will be able to speak directly to some people when you see them in the course of everyday affairs. You may need to telephone or write others.

Try to be as direct and specific as you can in your approach. One woman who wanted to change jobs knew many people in professional organizations. However, she saw them only once every few months at big national conferences. The first time, she said things like "I'm really glad you like your job. If you hear of anything like it, let me know" and "I wish I could find a way to leave *x* (her current company)." What happened as a result of this? Nothing. The second time she saw her friends, she said the same kind of things. "I'm ready for a change." "I wonder what I'll be doing a year from now." What happened? Nothing. Finally, she said to one friend who told her about an impending promotion, "If you get that job, I would be interested in working for you in your former position." Her friend, to whom she had made the other weak statements, was surprised to hear she was job hunting! What happened? She was invited to apply for the job when her friend's promotion came through. She said to others, "I'm looking for a new job, and I'm willing to relocate anywhere from New England to Washington, D.C." Since they all knew the kind of work she did, they did not have to ask more. What happened? People she had not even spoken to directly, in other words friends of friends, called her with suggestions and tips.

Professional associations have been mentioned before, and they need to be mentioned here again. Both national and local professional associations are extremely valuable in networking. If you are not currently working or are not working in the field you are trying to enter, a professional association provides a meeting ground on which it is perfectly acceptable to talk about business in a friendly, informal context. Attending meetings is an excellent way to extend your networks. In addition, many professional associations conduct placement services at their annual conventions.

One of the most important techniques for a job search is keeping records of what you have done and where it has led. This is particularly important in networking since one contact may lead to another. Here are the kind of records you can keep for networking.

Networking Records

Sample: Name: *Paul Bishop*
Address: *Ferry Road, Bristol, RI*
Telephone: *(401) 555-2664 (work)*
Source of contact: *friend of Aunt Louise*
Method of contact: *I telephoned him at work.*
Date(s) of contact: *2/17*
Results/follow-up: *He asked me to send him a résumé. Sent 2/19. Call him 2/28.*

Contact 1:   Name _____

Address _____

Telephone _____

Source of contact _____

Method of contact _____

Date(s) of contact _____

Results/follow-up _____

_____

_____

_____

Contact 2:   Name _____

Address _____

Telephone _____

Source of contact _____

Method of contact _____

Date(s) of contact _____

Results/follow-up _____

_____

_____

_____

Contact 3:   Name _____

Address _____

Telephone _____

Source of contact _____

Method of contact _____

Date(s) of contact _____

Results/follow-up _____

_____

_____

_____

Contact 4:   Name _____

Address _____

Telephone _____

Source of contact _____

Method of contact _____

Date(s) of contact _____

Results/follow-up _____

_____

_____

_____

Using professional employment services

Professional employment services are available from a variety of sources. If you are attending a school or college, your school probably has a placement office. If you have attended a college, you may be able to use the services of the placement office, often for a fee, even if you are no longer enrolled. State employment services also run employment offices. You can find these by looking under state listings in your local telephone directory. When you look at newspaper advertisements for jobs, you will see that many of them are placed by private employment agencies to which you can apply. In addition, if your company is going through a general staff reduction, it may have established an outplacement service. Finally, there are private career counseling services.

Although all of these services and agencies can be helpful to you in your job search, there are differences of which you should be aware. The placement office in your school works for you. You are the customer whether the service is free or not. Its interest is in placing you in the best job it can.

Employment agencies, on the other hand, work for companies with job vacancies. That is why there is no fee to you for placement. The fee is paid by the company. The agency's interest, therefore, is not in you but in finding the best possible person for the job. That does not mean that it will not be helpful to you. It does mean that you need to know its point of view. Some employment agencies that specialize in high-paying jobs are called executive search firms, or headhunters. They are usually interested only in highly experienced and qualified people. Therefore, if you are taking an unusual career path or just starting out, the headhunter type of agency will probably not be interested in you. Remember, this is not because you are not qualified. It is because the agency is working for the employer.

State employment services are more neutral. Their goal is to make as many placements as possible so that fewer people are unemployed and the economy of the state is healthy. The range of services provided by the state employment service varies from state to state. Outplacement services work for companies that are reducing their work force to help them place as many of those they will be letting go as possible. Outplacement services can be helpful to you in identifying new paths and in sharpening your job-hunting skills. However, do not feel the service is the only way you will find a new job. Private career counseling services work for you, the client. However, many of these career counseling services do not provide job placement. They help you assess your goals and develop résumé-writing and interviewing skills, the kind of skills presented in this book and others like it.

Find the employment service most suited to your needs. Use it to identify job leads and to get any help offered in presenting yourself on a job. You need not stick to one choice. You can use your company's outplacement service, register with your college placement office, and contact several employment agencies.

Answering advertisements

Answering advertisements often leads to job interviews. You can find job advertisements in your local newspaper in the classified section and often in specialized sections for business, education, and health. Several major newspapers, like the *New York Times* and *Wall Street Journal,* carry ads for national companies. If you are interested in working for a large organization, you might want to subscribe to one or both of these while you are job hunting. You will also find ads in professional newspapers and magazines for jobs related to the interests of the readers. For example, *ComputerWorld* lists programmer and analyst jobs.

Civil service job listings are another form of job advertising that will be useful if you are considering working in the public sector. Federal job information centers can give you information on jobs in the federal government that are located not only in Washington but in many places in the world. States and municipalities also provide civil service listings. While many civil service jobs require passing a test, others do not. They require that you have certain education or experience and that you apply with a résumé and follow-up interview, just as you would for private-sector jobs.

Advertising yourself

Advertising yourself takes some time and a little bit of money but is often effective, particularly in getting a first job. There are two techniques you can use. First, you can actually take out an advertisement. The best place to do this is in a newspaper, magazine, or professional journal that reaches the audience that might want to hire you. It should be a magazine that has a "situations wanted" section as a regular part of its classified advertisements. Otherwise, no one may know to look for your ad. The second technique is to carry out a large distribution of your résumé. You can identify the names for your résumé mailing list through the classified telephone directory or directories of business organizations such as *Standard & Poor's Register of Corporations, Directors and Executives, Dun and Bradstreet's Million Dollar Directory, Thomas Register of American Manufacturers, Bottin International Register, Fraser's Canadian-Trade Directory,* and others available to you in business libraries.

Checklist for Job Leads

Directions: Use this checklist to review the resources you have for identifying job leads. Place a check next to those you plan to use.

_____   1. Personal contacts with friends and relatives.

_____   2. Personal contacts with business associates.

_____   3. Personal contacts with teachers and professors, past and present.

_____   4. School and/or college placement office.

_____   5. State employment service.

_____   6. Private employment service.

_____   7. Executive search agencies (headhunters).

_____   8. Outplacement service.

_____   9. Professional association meetings.

_____   10. Professional association conference placement services.

_____   11. Professional or trade journals or newsletters.

_____   12. Classified telephone directories.

_____   13. Chamber of commerce lists.

_____   14. Federal job information centers.

_____   15. Directories of businesses.

Summary Checklist

In this chapter, you examined if and how you are going to move out of your current job. You considered whether you want to move up along the path you have been following or whether you prefer to move in a different direction altogether. Then you looked at some of the resources that can help you in your decision making and in putting your decisions to work once they have been made.

Use the checklist below to review your decisions.

_____ I have examined my reasons for wanting to leave my current job, and they are sound.

_____ I know the direction I next want to take. I will be looking for a job as _____

in an organization that _____

_____

_____

or

_____ I don't know the direction I want to take next, but I am going to follow this plan to figure it out:

_____

_____

_____

_____

_____ In looking for a job, I will find leads through the following sources:

_____

_____

_____

Making Your Résumé Work

Now that you have decided upon your next career move and identified some job leads, it is time to draft your winning résumé. The purpose of a winning résumé is to get you considered for a job. While it is not likely that anyone has ever gotten a job solely on the basis of her or his résumé, people do lose the chance to be considered because of poorly written or presented résumés. A résumé is often the first glimpse an employer has of your abilities, and it is also the written document that remains after the interactions of the interview have been carried off in the air.

The first section of this chapter summarizes the most important tips from employers on designing a winning résumé. The second section includes worksheets to help you begin your writing. The third section will help you get an attentive reading of your résumé through principles of rewriting, while the fourth section helps you arrange the résumé for a perfect finished copy. Both the third and fourth sections provide plenty of examples. In the fifth section, you will see what to include in a cover letter. The final section will help you establish a record-keeping system that will prove valuable in tracking your résumés and controlling your job search.

This chapter gives you some information about résumé writing. It would be silly to pretend, however, that this is all that can be said about résumés when there are many books on this subject alone. Much of the information in this chapter comes from *How to Write a Winning Résumé* (Deborah Perlmutter Bloch, VGM Career Horizons, 1989).

Tips from Employers on Winning Résumés

When employers in a variety of industries were asked to comment on good and bad points of résumé writing, they stressed the importance of relevant work experience; organization; brevity; and the presentation of factual, down-to-earth material. Some specific suggestions were:

"Make the résumé fit the job. There is no résumé that will fit every job."

"Spend a lot of time conveying what it is you want to say so that you can say it as concisely as possible. I like to see evidence that someone has put effort into communication."

"If I get a résumé of more than two pages from a young person, I'm getting fluff. Either the person can't write, or it's baloney."

"Be honest. Be factual. Avoid exaggeration at all costs."

"Don't try to create a false sense of drama and glory. The worst sin is when someone just out of college tries to make a big thing out of a part-time job and writes 'coordinated sanitary operations' when she kept the key to the ladies' room."

To get the kind of relevant, factual, well-organized résumé that draws employers' attention requires some work. Many people try to begin with the idea of the finished product in their heads. They try to summarize all of their experiences in the résumé format they picture without first thoroughly exploring those experiences. All too often, the effect is either a lengthy, rambling document or a brief outline that omits a lot of important material. Following the seven steps below will help you develop a winning résumé.

Seven steps to a winning résumé

1. Examine the relevant areas of your life in depth, making notes as you go. By writing out the details, you get the material that you need to write a comprehensive, convincing résumé. Worksheet spaces are provided in the pages that follow for you to develop this raw material.

2. Translate the details into the best language for a résumé. This language consists of action words, verbs, and vocabulary related to the field of work in which you are job hunting. You can look at the sample résumé in this chapter for some examples of this. If you are switching occupations or industries, you can also go to job descriptions in computer-based career information systems or in books to get a feel for the language of the field. If you are working with a counselor or other employment service, you can get help with this.

3. Select the parts of the résumé you want and write a rough draft of it.

4. Arrange your résumé on the page so that it is easy to read and attractive. You may need to type it several times until it looks the best it can.

5. Proofread your résumé. Eliminate all spelling and typographical errors. If you are not good at seeing spelling or usage errors, get help from someone who is. A résumé with errors, one that has sloppy corrections or black marks from photocopying, will not get you an interview. It makes it seem to the employers that you just don't care about working for them, or if you do care, that you can't tell a good job from a poor one.

6. Write a cover letter tailored to each specific employer to whom you are sending the résumé.

7. As you send résumés, begin to keep your résumé tracking records.

Beginning the Writing

This section of the chapter is designed to help you examine the relevant areas of your life in depth and provide a place for making notes as you do so. By writing out the details, you get the material that you need to write a comprehensive, convincing résumé.

The possible sections of a résumé are explained in the résumé worksheets. Use the blank spaces after each section to fill in information about yourself.

You will note as you look over the worksheets that there is no place for your age, marital status, or physical characteristics. That is because it is against the law to include these as factors in job selection. (Race, religion, and national origin are other factors that may not be considered. You will want to remember this in your interviews and throughout the job-hunting process.) Although you are permitted to give this information, many employers state that it seems inappropriate because it is no longer acceptable to choose people on the basis of these criteria.

You may also notice that there is no place for a job objective. That belongs in the cover letter, which will be explained in a later section in this chapter. There is also no place for a summary or highlights. The entire résumé is a summary.

Finally, you will see no place for references. In general, references are not listed on a résumé. However, if the advertisement or job posting you are responding to calls for references, list current or former supervisors, colleagues, teachers or professors, or others with whom you have a business relationship. Be sure to secure permission from those you have listed before sending out your résumé. If your references are on file with a school or college placement office, you may make a statement like this one: References are available from: Placement Office, ABC University, 1234 Fifth Street, Toledo, Ohio 43716.

Résumé Worksheet 1—The Heading

Directions: The heading is an essential section. It must include your name, home address, and telephone number. If you can receive calls at work, include your business number. This makes it easier for people to reach you during their business day.

Name _____

Full Address _____

_____

_____

Home telephone number _____

Office telephone number _____

Résumé Worksheet 2—Education

Directions: Education is also an essential section. Include the degrees you have earned, the institutions at which you earned them, and the dates of attendance. List your most advanced degree first. You should also list any courses taken to upgrade or enhance your skills. Finally, if you were awarded any honors in school, list them.

School name _____

Dates attended: from _____ to _____

Type of diploma _____

Major _____

Special projects _____

_____

_____

Evidence of leadership _____

_____

_____

Awards or honors _____

School name _____

Dates attended: from _____ to _____

Type of diploma _____

Major _____

Special projects _____

_____

_____

Evidence of leadership _____

_____

_____

Awards or honors _____

School name _____

   Dates attended: from _____ to _____

   Type of diploma _____

   Major (if any) _____

   Special projects _____

   _____

   _____

   Evidence of leadership _____

   _____

   _____

   Awards or honors _____

Other courses, seminars, or special training

_____

_____

_____

_____

_____

_____

_____

Résumé Worksheet 3—Work History

Directions: This is the most essential section and should include each of your jobs, beginning with the most recent. The more recent jobs should have more detail and get more space in the finished copy.

Job 1: Name of company or organization _____

Address _____

Type of work _____

Dates of employment _____

Major duties and responsibilities _____

_____

_____

Most important accomplishments _____

_____

_____

Job 2: Name of company or organization _____

Address _____

Type of work _____

Dates of employment _____

Major duties and responsibilities _____

_____

_____

Most important accomplishments _____

_____

_____

Job 3: Name of company or organization _____

    Address _____

    Type of work _____

    Dates of employment _____

    Major duties and responsibilities _____

    _____

    _____

    Most important accomplishments _____

    _____

    _____

Job 4: Name of company or organization _____

    Address _____

    Type of work _____

    Dates of employment _____

    Major duties and responsibilities _____

    _____

    Most important accomplishments _____

    _____

Job 5: Name of company or organization _____

    Address _____

    Type of work _____

    Dates of employment _____

    Major duties and responsibilities _____

    _____

    Most important accomplishments _____

    _____

Résumé Worksheet 4—Licenses and Certificates

Directions: "Professional licenses and certificates" is an essential section if these are required for the kind of work you do. Give the title, issuing agency, and date of issuance for each license you hold.

License 1:

Title of license _____

Issued by _____

Date of issue _____

License 2:

Title of license _____

Issued by _____

Date of issue _____

License 3:

Title of license _____

Issued by _____

Date of issue _____

License 4:

Title of license _____

Issued by _____

Date of issue _____

License 5:

Title of license _____

Issued by _____

Date of issue _____

Résumé Worksheet 5—Related Experience

Directions: "Related Experience" is an optional section. It is helpful to have this section if you have work experience that is important to the job you are seeking but does not fit neatly into your work history. This might include experiences like consulting or teaching. Again, you will want to list what you did, where you did it, and when you did it.

Related Experience 1:

Name of company or organization _____

Type of work _____

Dates of work _____

Major duties and responsibilities _____

_____

Most important accomplishments _____

_____

_____

Related Experience 2:

Name of company or organization _____

Type of work _____

Dates of work _____

Major duties and responsibilities _____

_____

Most important accomplishments _____

_____

_____

Related Experience 3:

Name of company or organization _____

Type of work _____

Dates of work _____

Major duties and responsibilities _____

_____

Most important accomplishments _____

_____

_____

Related Experience 4:

Name of company or organization _____

Type of work _____

Dates of work _____

Major duties and responsibilities _____

_____

Most important accomplishments _____

_____

_____

Related Experience 5:

Name of company or organization _____

Type of work _____

Dates of work _____

Major duties and responsibilities _____

_____

Most important accomplishments _____

_____

_____

Résumé Worksheet 6—Professional Association, Leisure, and Volunteer Activities

Directions: "Professional Association, Leisure, and Volunteer Activities" should be included only if you have activities that show enthusiasm, energy, and a high level of interest. These are characteristics employers like. However, if your hobbies are only of passing interest to you, do not include this section. When the potential employer starts to talk to you about them in the interview, your lack of real interest will be against you. Use this section to show work that you have done for which you have not been paid or to show hobbies or sports that are really important to you. Be sure to include professional associations if you have held office.

Professional Association Activities: _____

_____

_____

_____

_____

_____

Leisure Activities: _____

_____

_____

_____

_____

_____

Volunteer Activities: _____

_____

_____

_____

_____

_____

Résumé Worksheet 7—Special Abilities

Directions: "Special Abilities" is an optional section that you will include if you have abilities related to your work such as a knowledge of foreign languages. In general, these are listed after the work history. However, if you are looking for a job in the computer field, your knowledge of programming languages and computer systems should be the first item after the heading.

_____

_____

_____

_____

_____

_____

_____

_____

_____

_____

_____

_____

_____

_____

_____

_____

_____

Résumé Worksheet 8—Publications and Presentations

Directions: This optional section should be included if you have any publications or presentations. If you believe the list will make your résumé too long, make a statement within the résumé and attach the list at the end. A statement might read: ''Twelve related publications in national journals and fifteen recent presentations at national and regional conferences are listed on the attachment to this résumé.''

For each publication or presentation, be sure to include the name of the journal or conference, the month and year of publication or presentation, and any coauthors or copresenters.

Name of your presentation or article _____

Journal or conference _____

Place of conference _____

Date of publication or presentation _____

Coauthors or copresenters _____

Name of your presentation or article _____

Journal or conference _____

Place of conference _____

Date of publication or presentation _____

Coauthors or copresenters _____

Name of your presentation or article _____

Journal or conference _____

Place of conference _____

Date of publication or presentation _____

Coauthors or copresenters _____

Name of your presentation or article _____

Journal or conference _____

Place of conference _____

Date of publication or presentation _____

Coauthors or copresenters _____

Rewriting for the Reader's Attention

In interviews with personnel officers, it was clear that what most impresses them in winning résumés is the forthright statement of what the job applicant has accomplished. The first thing that all the interviewers said they looked for was what people had done in their previous work. They all said that they were looking for experience directly connected to the job they were trying to fill.

In this section, you will take the statements you made about yourself in the résumé worksheets and translate them into the words that your readers—people with the power to consider you for a job—are looking for. Two methods are included. The first method involves taking your statements from sections of the résumé worksheets and rephrasing them with action words, or verbs. The second method involves your translating your experiences into the language of the job for which you are applying.

Method 1: Use action words

Action words are verbs. One way to identify a verb is by the fact that it can usually take an "-ed" ending to form the past tense. Some verbs have familiar irregular forms for the past. We say "wrote" for the past tense of the verb *write*, not "writted." Another way to identify a verb is to try to use the word *I* in front of it. To help you, a list of verbs in the past or "-ed" form is given below. Of course these are not the only verbs you may use, nor will you be able to use all of them. Some verbs that may be useful to you in writing your résumé follow.

Useful verbs for résumé writing

analyzed	handled
assumed responsibility	implemented
billed	improved
carried out	maintained
communicated	managed
completed	operated
coordinated	produced
designed	reduced costs
determined	saved
developed	supervised
documented	trained
established	wrote
gathered	

Review the list of verbs. Circle those that represent actions you have taken. Add some of your own. Now take the statements you made in the work history, related experience, and volunteer and leisure activities worksheets. Rewrite your responsibilities, special projects, and accomplishments to stress your actions—use a verb to begin each statement. You will need to use some separate sheets of paper to do this. An example follows.

Sample of Rewriting Using Verbs

This is the information that was recorded on the work history worksheet.

Type of work: Attorney

Major duties and responsibilities: Diversified legal and tax practice. Outside counsel for ABC Title Co. Representative for accountants and their clients before the IRS and tax courts. Close for several title companies.

Most important accomplishments: Coordinator and co-sponsor of a semiannual seminar for newly admitted attorneys. I managed my own practice. I taught at Brooklyn Law School.

Here is the rewritten description using verbs. See how much more action oriented it is.

> Developed and directed diversified law and tax practice. Served as outside counsel to ABC Title Co. Conducted closings for several title companies. Represented clients and accountants before the Internal Revenue Service and tax courts. Coordinated and sponsored a semiannual seminar for newly admitted attorneys. Taught law and taxation, as adjunct professor, at Brooklyn Law School.

Method 2: Translate your experiences into job-related language

Every job and industry has a special vocabulary, or jargon, a way of using words that is unique to that field. Another way of catching and holding the interest of the reader of your résumé is to use the words the reader expects to see.

In the previous chapter, you saw how to find job descriptions through interviews and reading. Use those descriptions now to rewrite the material in your résumé worksheets so that it captures the language of the job and field that interest you. This method of rewriting your personal history is particularly useful if you are trying to change careers or enter the job market for the first time.

Sample of Rewriting Using Job-Related Language

This is the information that was recorded on the work history worksheet of a recent college graduate who held a summer job as a supervising field interviewer for a citizens' action group.

> I helped citizens become aware of the state legislative process and issues of toxic waste, utility control, and consumer legislation. I helped the field interviewers communicate better with the citizens. I was responsible for developing and maintaining motivation among the employees and for supervising their work.

Here is a job description for public administrator:

> *Responsibilities:* Coordinate and direct public services to meet the needs of the nation, state, or community. Analyze problems; work with special committees and public agencies; recommend solutions to governing bodies.
> *Aptitudes and Skills:* Ability to relate to and communicate with people; solve complex problems through analysis; plan, organize, and implement policies and programs. Knowledge of political systems; financial management; personnel administration; program evaluation; organizational theory.

This is the rewritten description of the same accomplishments.

> Wrote pamphlets and conducted discussion groups to inform citizens of legislative processes and consumer issues. Organized and supervised crew of interviewers. Trained interviewers in effective communication skills.

Now it is your turn to rewrite your worksheets using job-related language. In doing this, please remember to continue to use the action words discussed in the previous portion of this chapter.

Producing a Perfect Finished Résumé

In interviews with personnel officers, it became clear that there was no particular style or paper that was preferable. What emerged from the discussions was the overwhelming importance of neatness and "good grooming" in a résumé. Some of the worst sins in résumé presentation were sloppiness, misspellings, thumb smudges, hand corrections, and whiting out. One personnel officer summed it up when he said "A piece of paper that has not been taken care of shows disdain for the reader, the process, and the job applicant himself." Others said that since attention to detail was important to their field, lack of attention to detail in a résumé showed them that an applicant could probably not do the job at hand. While there is no single appropriate layout that will fit every résumé, there are some good rules to follow.

Four good rules for résumé layout

1. Leave a one-inch margin all around the page to frame the information.

2. Use spacing between lines and indentations of material to draw attention to important facts. Do not cram everything together.

3. Be consistent in the type of headings you use. For example, if you capitalize the heading EDUCATION, do not use initial capital letters and underlining for the equal heading <u>Job Experience</u>.

4. Try to get your résumé on one page. If your experience is extensive and you cannot get it on one page, try to arrange your material so that the most important items appear on the first page.

Two résumés follow. The first is an example of a chronological résumé in a good, standard layout. Employers generally prefer this layout because they can then easily compare the education and experience of one worker to another. They can also easily see the chronology of the work.

The second is an example of a functional résumé. Use the functional résumé only if the chronological résumé cannot fit your work experience. This may be true because you have been homemaking or working in another unpaid position for some time. It may also be true because you are shifting on your career path from one type of job or industry to another.

It may take several tries until you have your résumé laid out to make the most of the presentation. This does not require any special typing facilities such as bold type or italics, although they may be used. However, if you have access to a word processor, using it can make rearranging easier.

Once you have the résumé in the form in which you want it, be sure to proofread it for spelling and usage errors. It is always a good idea to have at least one other person proofread it as well.

It is not necessarily a good idea to have your résumé photocopied in bulk unless you have immediate plans for a broadcast mailing. A broadcast mailing means that you send your résumé, unasked for, to many organizations within the industry that interests you. You can identify these organizations through listings in the classified telephone directory or in the business directories mentioned earlier. It is much better to have your résumé on a word processor so that you can make slight adjustments to fit each job for which you apply. Whether you photocopy it, type it, or print it out for each mailing, be sure the paper is free of smudges and the copy is straight on the paper. It is a shame to lose the benefits of all of your hard work in these simple details. But the employers certainly said over and over, in many ways, that neatness counts!

Chronological Résumé

Donald Jensen
4123 Smooth Way
St. Paul, Minnesota 55101
(612) 555-1234

EDUCATION

1970   Baruch College–City University of New York. BBA—Accounting.

1975   University of Minnesota—JD
University of Minnesota School of Law—Additional graduate courses in law of taxation.

EXPERIENCE

1985 to present   ***Stork Company   Minneapolis, MN***
Assistant Director of Taxes and Tax Counsel
- Advised management of the tax consequences of prospective acquisitions, mergers, liquidations, and operational transactions and proposed alternatives to maximize tax savings.
- Monitored proposed tax legislation, developed the company position for or against specific provisions, and communicated with tax legislative and regulatory staff through industry and professional association spokesmen.
- Established and updated procedures for ensuring compliance with changes in tax laws, created a microcomputer spread sheet system to assist in the preparation of tax returns.
- Supervised the preparation of all tax returns and reviewed filings for technical compliance with tax laws.
- Reviewed foreign subsidiary tax returns and recommended foreign dividend payments which maximized utilization of foreign tax credits.
- Reviewed income tax provisions for financial statements and documented the variances between the financial and tax return treatment of transactions.
- Represented the company before the I.R.S. and state and local taxing authorities on audits and post-audit administrative reviews and participated with retained counsel in tax litigations.
- Participated in industry and professional association tax committees in a leadership role.

1980–1985   ***Holt Industries, Inc.   St. Paul, MN***
Tax Attorney
- Directed research and planning for domestic and foreign transactions, including acquisitions, liquidations, leases, ruling requests, and extensive analyses of depreciation and tax credit issues.
- Participated in federal and state tax audits to advocate the company position on matters in issue.
- Prepared and filed protests for administrative reviews and assisted outside counsel in tax litigation.

1975–1980   ***Pan-Pacific Airlines, Inc.   New York, NY***
Tax Attorney, International
- Reviewed foreign tax returns and prepared U.S. Form 1118 for foreign tax credits.
- Managed the tax equalization program for U.S. nationals employed overseas.

PROFESSIONAL AFFILIATIONS

- Admitted to practice before the U.S. Tax Court, the Court of Claims, and the Minnesota courts.
- Member of the American Bar Association—Section on Taxation, the Minnesota State Bar Association, and the Minneapolis Bar Association.
- Past vice president and former chairman of the Federal Tax Committee of the American Tax Executives Institute.

Functional Résumé

(for an individual trying to move from a career in the schools to a job in training and development in a corporate environment)

Harold Grayson
1235 Elm Street
Dover, Delaware 19807
Home Telephone: (302) 555-7112
Office Telephone: (302) 555-1200

EXPERIENCE

MANAGEMENT
Developed and implemented programs to improve staff morale and delivery of services and to facilitate orientation of people new to the organization. Administered training programs in basic skills. Supervised the work of three people in an office offering counseling services to more than eight hundred clients per year. Served as liaison to external organizations. Published and disseminated in-house organs on events related to career development.

PLACEMENT
AND
DEVELOPMENT
Counseled unemployed clients in a training program for the purposes of job placement. Provided supportive counseling services to clients while they trained for employment. Conducted individual counseling, small-group seminars, and large-audience presentations.

TRAINING
Trained staff in career orientation, placement, and counseling skills. Developed and delivered programs to improve clients' communications and job-seeking skills. Developed programs in basic learning skills.

EDUCATION

University of Wisconsin–Madison, B.A., History, 1978

University of Wisconsin–Madison, M.S., Counseling, 1982 and Advanced Certificate, Counseling, 1983

PROFESSIONAL AFFILIATIONS

Association for Training and Development
American Psychological Association
American Association for Counseling and Development

WORK HISTORY

1989—present (summers)	Training Supervisor, G. T. and E. Corporation
1987—1988 (summers)	Trainer, G. T. and E. Corporation: Job
	Training Partnership Act Program
1983—present	Counselor, Madison Public High Schools
1978—1983	Social studies teacher, Madison Public High School

Writing a Cover Letter   Now that you have finished your résumé, you need to prepare a cover letter. It tells employers why you are sending them your résumé. Remember that the cover letter is designed to introduce the résumé and interest your potential employer in reading your résumé, just as the résumé is designed to interest that person in meeting you. Like the résumé, the cover letter must be neat and clean in both content and production. There are seven essential sections of the cover letter.

Seven sections of the cover letter

1. Your address (unless it is typed on your personal letterhead, which already includes this information).

2. The date.

3. The inside address of the person and company to whom you are sending the résumé. If you are addressing a box number in an advertisement, include the box number information and then the line "To whom it may concern:."

4. The first paragraph should explain why you are writing this letter. Is it in response to an advertisement, the result of a previous meeting, or at the suggestion of someone who is helping you through your networking contacts?

5. The second paragraph should present one or two highlights of your experience in terms of what you believe to be the requirements of the job or needs of the company.

6. The final paragraph should close with a request for an interview and any pertinent information needed to schedule the interview. This might include hours at which you can be reached at a particular telephone number.

7. Whether the letter is to a classified ad box or to an individual, the correct closing is, "Sincerely," or "Yours truly," followed by your signature, followed by your full name typed out.

The cover letter must always be an individually typed, one-page document on good, 8 1/2-by-11-inch bond paper. Since cover letters must be written to particular individuals, or at least to particular companies, they cannot be reproduced or photocopied like résumés. Of course once you have written and rewritten your first cover letter to the point where you really like it, you may certainly use the same or similar wording in subsequent letters.

After you have typed your cover letter, proofread it as thoroughly as you did the résumé. Handle it carefully to avoid a dirty appearance. Mail the cover letter and résumé in an envelope of the appropriate size.

A sample of a good cover letter follows.

Sample Cover Letter

South Hollow Road
Hoosick Falls, New York 12090
August 11, 1990

Mr. Thomas Feigen
Cantwell Computer Company
1212 North Street
Pittsfield, Massachusetts 01201

Dear Mr. Feigen:

I have enclosed my résumé in application for the job as a computer salesperson which you advertised in The Berkshire Eagle of August 9th.

My résumé summarizes my experiences in sales of office equipment to small companies and my knowledge of computers as an active and interested user of PCs for the past four years. I believe that both of these areas of expertise will ensure my success in sales for your organization.

I look forward to meeting with you at your convenience to discuss how I could fit into your company's sales team. I can be reached during the day at (518) 555-3100 or in the evenings at (518) 555-9867.

Yours truly,

Susan Green

Susan Green

Tracking the Results of Your Résumé

Making the right career moves is a challenging and time-consuming process. You want to be sure that you are always moving forward, not going back on your own tracks or around in circles. At the beginning of the process, you may feel exhilarated and think you could never forget any of the letters you have sent or what to do to follow up. However, unless you meet with unusually quick success, you will need to have records of what you have done.

A good place to begin is by keeping track of résumés as you send them or give them out. You can build on your résumé tracking record as you go for interviews and begin to have ongoing dialogues with some organizations. The higher the position you are seeking, the more likely it is that you will have several contacts with people in the organization before you are hired.

One method of record keeping is to make photocopies of your cover letters and note any response and interviews on them. Another method is to use the outline below. You can use large index cards, one for each résumé sent, or individual sheets kept in a notebook or folder. A completed sample record is shown, followed by a blank for making copies for your use.

Résumé Tracking Record

Sample

Sent To:
Company name Sonotext Systems, Inc.
Name of individual George B. Hayes
Title Vice President
Address 4044 Congress Avenue
City, state, zip Austin, TX 78778
Telephone (512) 555-1096
Date sent 11/28/89

Results:
Date 2/17/90 first interview; 3/11/90 recalled.
Names Saw Eugene H. Perler; George B. Hayes; Marilyn Mayle. Perler appears to be the decision maker because it is his department. Place of Mayle in decision is unclear.
Action Had two interviews; wrote thank-you notes; still seems a possible opening.
Follow-up Call Hayes in two months, 5/11/90.

Sent To: Company _____

Name of individual (if known) _____

Title _____

Address _____

City, state, zip _____

Telephone _____

Date sent _____

Results: Date _____

Names _____

_____

Action _____

_____

Follow-up (if any) _____

_____

Summary Checklist

In this chapter, you worked on constructing your résumé, preparing it for mailing, and recording the results. Use the checklist below to be sure you have carried out all the steps that ensure a winning résumé.

_____ I have examined the relevant areas of my life in depth and made notes about them.

_____ I have translated the details from my notes into the best language for a résumé—action words and job-related vocabulary.

_____ I have selected the parts of the résumé I want and written a rough draft of it.

_____ I have arranged my résumé on the page so that it is easy to read and attractive.

_____ I have proofread my résumé, eliminating all spelling and typographical errors.

_____ I have written or I am prepared to write a cover letter tailored to each specific employer to whom I am sending the résumé.

_____ I have begun or I am ready to begin to keep résumé tracking records.

Winning Interviews

Once you have identified the jobs that interest you and you have begun networking and sending résumés, you can expect to be called for interviews. This chapter will take you through the seven steps to a winning interview, an interview that gets you the job you want. It is important to know from the beginning that it is highly unlikely that you will get the first job you are interviewed for. Most people go through many interviews before they get the right job. Many of them report, however, that they get better and better at it with practice.

Much of the information in this chapter came from discussions with employers in a variety of industries including advertising, accounting, banking, merchandising, and computers. They stressed the importance of preparing for an interview so that you can present your skills and experiences in a way that has meaning for the employer. The seven steps will help you do that.

It is important to remember that an interview is not a contest between you and the employer. A winning interview means that you both end up on the same team. Listed below are the seven steps that will put you on the winning team. The rest of the chapter gives you more information on how to carry out each of the steps and provides you with worksheets that will help you in your preparation.

Seven steps to a winning interview

1. Assess your own strengths and weaknesses.
2. Learn all you can about the job and the company or organization to which you are applying.
3. Think about how your skills fit the job and how you can benefit the company or organization.
4. Know the kinds of questions you will probably be asked and how to answer them.
5. Know the questions you want to ask and when to ask them.
6. Accept your nervousness and turn nervous energy into positive energy.
7. Track the results of your interviews.

Assess Your Strengths and Weaknesses

Before you can go into the interview and let someone else know what your strengths are and how you can overcome any weaknesses that you have, you have to understand them yourself. Just as you had to think through information on your background to prepare your résumé, you have to do some analysis before the job interview. Once you have done this, you will be ready to think about the skills that are needed on the job you are seeking and match your skills to those needed.

There are three worksheets on the pages that follow. The first one asks you to think of skills you have developed in various activities in your life. The second gives a list of traits that employers said they found important. You are asked to think of whether you have this trait and what examples you have from any area of your life that demonstrate you have it. The last worksheet in this section asks you to assess honestly any weaknesses you have and how you can overcome them. In all of this, try to think of strengths and weaknesses as they relate to the kind of job you are looking for.

Strength Assessment Worksheet 1

I have acquired the following job skills through education:

Skill   **Course**

Example: know spreadsheets   took courses at community college

_____   _____

_____   _____

_____   _____

_____   _____

I have acquired the following job skills at work:

Skill   **Job Responsibility**

Example: budgeting   developed annual program budget

_____   _____

_____   _____

_____   _____

_____   _____

I have acquired the following job skills in professional, volunteer, or leisure activities:

Skill   **Activity**

Example: persuasion   collected funds for the Red Cross

_____   _____

_____   _____

_____   _____

Strength Assessment Worksheet 2

Directions: Listed below are ten traits. Put a check next to each one that is true of you and describe how you used each trait in some work, school, or other activity.

Trait	Activity
_____ Teamworker	_____
	_____
_____ Tactful	_____
	_____
_____ Adaptable to change	_____
	_____
_____ Show initiative	_____
	_____
_____ Self-disciplined	_____
	_____
_____ Conscientious	_____
	_____
_____ Hard worker	_____
	_____
_____ Honest and sincere	_____
	_____
_____ Able to think	_____
	_____
_____ Self-motivated	_____
	_____

Strength Assessment Worksheet 3

Directions: What do you consider your three greatest weaknesses, and how are you working to overcome them? (Knowing your weaknesses, not pretending you are Superman or Wonder Woman, helps you identify your strengths.)

Weakness

I am overcoming it by:

Example: losing my temper

learning to count to ten

1. _____   _____

   _____   _____

   _____   _____

2. _____   _____

   _____   _____

   _____   _____

3. _____   _____

   _____   _____

   _____   _____

4. _____   _____

   _____   _____

   _____   _____

5. _____   _____

   _____   _____

   _____   _____

Learn about the Job   Before you go for a job interview, you need to be able to look at things from an employer's point of view. Looking at things from the employer's point of view will help you answer questions so that they are meaningful to her or him. In the job interview, the right answer always centers on the job and how you relate to it.

If you are using any of the employment services discussed in chapter 4, you can get help from them in getting information about the jobs you are applying for and about the company or organizations that are offering these jobs. You can also use the general sources in the library that have been mentioned—computer-based career information delivery systems, printed information that describes jobs in general, annual reports of corporations, and business directories. If you know anyone who is in a similar job or who works for the company to which you will be applying, talk to that person for information.

The job information worksheet gives you an idea of the kinds of questions you will want to know about each job. You may want to duplicate the worksheet before you fill it in since you will probably apply for more than one job before you are offered one that you accept.

Job Information Worksheet

1. What is the major product or service of this organization?

_____

_____

2. How does the job I am seeking contribute to this product or service?

_____

_____

_____

_____

3. What are the major responsibilities of the job I am seeking?

_____

_____

_____

4. What skills or knowledge does someone need to carry out these responsibilities?

_____

_____

_____

5. Which of these skills or knowledge do I have?

_____

_____

_____

Match Your Skills to the Job

When you filled in the job information worksheet, you began to think about how your skills and knowledge fit the job you are seeking. In the worksheet that follows, you will bring together what you have learned about yourself and about the job. Bringing these together and concentrating on them in giving your answers will produce a winning interview. Sometimes employers ask general questions like "What can you tell me about yourself?" They really want to know about you in relation to their job. This is an opportunity to take information from the job match worksheet that follows and talk about it.

You will need to think about the job requirements in three general areas: educational requirements, technical skills, and knowledge and interpersonal skills. An example of an educational requirement is the need for a degree in accounting. An example of a technical skill is the ability to conduct a needs assessment. An example of an interpersonal skill is the abilty to communicate in writing with people of varied educational backgrounds.

Job Match Worksheet

Educational Requirements   **My Qualifications**   **Proof**

_____   _____   _____
_____   _____   _____
_____   _____   _____
_____   _____   _____
_____   _____   _____
_____   _____   _____

Technical Requirements   **My Qualifications**   **Proof**

_____   _____   _____
_____   _____   _____
_____   _____   _____
_____   _____   _____
_____   _____   _____
_____   _____   _____

Interpersonal Requirements   **My Qualifications**   **Proof**

_____   _____   _____
_____   _____   _____
_____   _____   _____
_____   _____   _____
_____   _____   _____
_____   _____   _____

In addition to considering how you will fit into the occupation, you will want to think ahead of time about how you fit into the organization—how your work can benefit it. Of course you also expect to derive benefits, but in an interview, the focus is on your service to the company. In addition, thinking about how you will fit into the organization will prepare you to frame your answers in the vocabulary of that field. For example, if you have applied for a job as a counselor in an agency, you want to talk about clients. On the other hand, if you are looking for a job in a school, it would be better if you spoke about students.

Use the questions in the organizational fit worksheet to prepare for each interview. Again, you will probably want to make copies of this worksheet for preparation for different interviews.

Organizational Fit Worksheet

1. What is the major product or service of this organization?

_____

_____

_____

_____

_____

2. How does the job I am seeking contribute to the product or service?

_____

_____

_____

_____

_____

3. What are some of the goals of the organization or of the industry at large?

_____

_____

_____

_____

_____

4. How can my skills contribute to reaching these goals?

_____

_____

_____

_____

_____

5. What are some of the current problems in this organization or industry?

_____

_____

_____

_____

_____

6. How can I contribute to the solution?

_____

_____

_____

_____

7. What are some of the changes in the industry or workplace that can be expected in the next five years?

_____

_____

_____

_____

8. How will I adapt to these changes?

_____

_____

_____

_____

Give the Right Answers   If you think about the kinds of questions you will be asked ahead of time, it is easier to be prepared with the answers you want to give. There are three basic kinds of questions employers will ask.

Three types of interview questions

1. The specific question. Examples include:
   "What was your most important responsibility on your last job?"
   "What did you like best (or least) about the jobs you have held?"
   "What were your major courses of study?"
   "Why did you choose those courses?"
   "What did you learn in (some experience on your résumé)?"
   "How do you see yourself fitting in with this job?" (after a description of the job)
2. The general question. Examples include:
   "What can you tell me about yourself?"
   "Why do you think you are the best person for this job?"
   "Why do you want this job?"
   "Is there anything else that you would like me to know?"
3. The problem question. In this type of question, the employer describes a situation that you might come across on the job and asks you how you would handle it.

You can expect questions not just about the facts of your education, job experience, and interests but about your attitudes and feelings toward them. The interviewers will probably ask some questions about how you feel about their company. They may ask questions about your future plans to try to assess your commitment to their job or company. You may also expect to have questions that indicate whether you know your work and are up-to-date in the field. These are the hardest questions to find in any textbook or to put on a list because they are different for every job.

To answer a specific question, be specific. Give details of your experience and accomplishments. As much as possible, relate these to the job you are interviewing for.

When asked a general question, you have to make a series of quick choices. First, you have to decide whether to answer the question or ask a question about it. If the interviewer says, for example, "Tell me about your background," you can ask, "Would you like me to start with my education or my work experience?" On the other hand, you can use that opportunity to point up your strengths, knowledge of the job, and information about the company. As soon as you have made the choice to answer the question, you have to decide where in your background to begin. As often as possible, try to use general responses to give the information you decided you wanted to communicate in your analysis of strengths. Of course if a question is really vague and you have no idea what the interviewer means, ask for help.

When you are asked a problem-solving question, the first thing to do is think. Don't be afraid to take some time to plan your answer. The interviewer will respect you more. Try to hear the entire problem when it is first presented, but if it is complicated and you have missed some part, ask to have it repeated.

Answer as if you were already in the job. Do not speak as if you are an outside expert or a student but as if you are already the person in place. Remember that you are part of an organization. One of the key questions in the interviewer's mind is, "Do I want this person on my team?" While you do not want to go running to your boss too quickly, you also do not want to seem to be taking on the whole world by yourself.

Remember your strengths that you identified on the worksheets in this chapter. Remember how they match the skills and knowledge this job requires. Use that information in answering any type of question.

You also identified weaknesses on your worksheets. Understanding your own weaknesses will help you with your answers when one of them is brought up in an interview. It is important that you be honest about your background but not that you make it worse than it is. Remember the difference between discretion and dishonesty. Discretion means that you do not have to reveal all your thoughts about yourself or anyone else. You do not have to say that you left a job "because it was boring, boring, boring!" Better to say that you left it for a more challenging opportunity. You cannot, however, say that you graduated from college if you did not. The first is a good use of discretion. The second is dishonest.

Know the questions you do not have to answer. There are a number of areas about which an employer may not ask questions as defined by the United States Constitution, federal laws, and court decisions. There are four areas of questions forbidden to employers—questions about your race, religion, or ethnic origins; questions about your age; questions about your marital status or children; and questions about your height, weight, health, and handicapping conditions unless these are related to specific job requirements.

Ask the Right Questions at the Right Time

The key to using questions for a winning interview is when to ask the questions. We asked the employers we interviewed what questions they found appropriate and which ones they found inappropriate. Here are some of their answers:

> I like when people ask about the size of our organization and their opportunity for advancement in it. I like them to ask about their duties and the kinds of clients they'll be dealing with. Of course, they need to know about benefits and vacation too.

> I like a candidate to ask questions that show he or she has done his or her research. For example, 'What age group will I be dealing with?' 'What kind of students will I be teaching?' I like task-related questions.

> I don't like questions that imply a person will be watching the clock and leaving at the first possible minute—'How much money will I make?' 'What are the hours?'

> The worst thing someone can ask about is hours—'Is there much homework?' As far as the company is concerned, they can't put in too many hours. If it means they have to work on a weekend, let them work. Any question about workload is the end for that applicant.

An analysis of employers' feelings about questions is consistent with everything else they have said. They want someone who is strongly interested in doing the job for their organization. They want you if you want the job, not its benefits. Of course work is an economic activity. Everyone knows that salary and benefits are important, but the most important thing, according to the employers, is the work itself, the job of the job. This means you have to ask the right questions at the right time.

Do not ask about salary or benefits until you are offered a job or the interviewer brings it up. Although this information may be of vital interest to you, remember to picture the interview from the employer's point of view. You are selling your services to the employer. The employer is not sure that she or he wants to buy them. If you were selling a valuable object, you would not begin with its price tag!

Once you have been offered a job, you can ask what the salary or salary range of the job is. At that time, you may also ask about any benefits that are important to you and appropriate to the job. If particular benefits will not make a difference in whether you accept a job, it is best that you do not ask about them until after you are hired since salary and benefits are often a matter of overall negotiation.

Salary and Benefits Question Worksheet

Directions: Look at the questions about salary and benefits. Decide which ones are essential to you, the ones you must know about before you accept a job. Put a star next to them. Put a check next to those you will ask after accepting employment. Cross out any items of no interest to you. You will also see space for some questions of your own.

_____ 1. What is my starting salary?

_____ 2. How are salary increases determined?

_____ 3. What kind of health insurance plan can I get?

_____ 4. Who pays for the health insurance?

_____ 5. Is there a dental benefits plan?

_____ 6. Is there any reimbursement for college or graduate school expense?

_____ 7. How will I be reimbursed for work-related travel expenses?

_____ 8. Does this position qualify for stock options?

_____ 9. Does this position include a company car?

_____ 10. How much does the company pay for relocation expenses?

_____ 11. What is my total compensation package?

_____ 12. How many vacation days do I get a year?

_____ 13. What restrictions are there, if any, on taking vacation?

_____ 14. What is the organization's sick leave policy?

_____ 15. What hours will I work?

_____ 16. Is there overtime pay or compensatory time off?

_____ 17. _____

_____ 18. _____

_____ 19. _____

_____ 20. _____

_____ 21. _____

_____ 22. _____

_____ 23. _____

_____ 24. _____

_____ 25. _____

The employer may bring up the question of salary during the interview process. There are generally three ways in which the employer can ask you about salary. You need to be prepared to answer each of these questions:

1. *What salary are you willing to accept?*   If you are an experienced worker, you probably know the answer to this question, based on your previous jobs. If you are just starting out in an occupation, it is important that you do your research and have some idea of the salaries being offered in your field. Giving a realistic response shows your knowledge.

2. *What is your current salary?*   Your answer to this question can vary with your goals. If you feel your current salary is in line with the industry wage for your job, you can give an exact figure: "$35,000." If you want to be somewhat more general, you can say "the mid-thirties." If your current salary is too low and you really will not move unless you get something considerably higher, you can answer the question that wasn't asked and say "My minimum salary requirement to move is $40,000."

3. *The salary range for this job is $32,000 to $35,000. How does that sound to you?* Your answer should indicate either that the range is acceptable or unacceptable. If you believe it is too low, you can ask how the range is determined and what the next range is. If you feel you qualify for the next range, you can then say why this is so.

Asking questions about the nature of the work you will be doing and about the organization itself is appropriate during the interview. One word of caution: these questions show interest only if you are really interested in the answer. Most of us are not accomplished actors. We cannot convince other people that we feel something we do not feel.

Job Question Worksheet

Directions: Listed below are some good job-related questions. Put a star next to the ones you would like to ask in an interview. Space is also provided for your own questions.

_____   1. What will be the major responsibilities of this job?

_____   2. Where does this job fit in the overall organization?

_____   3. In which location will I work?

_____   4. What specific projects do you see me starting first?

_____   5. What is a typical career path from this job in your company?

_____   6. Why did the person previously in the job leave?

_____   7. Who will be my immediate supervisor? Can I meet her or him?

_____   8. Your annual reports show steady growth over the last three years. How rapidly do you plan to grow over the next three years?

_____   9. Are there particular customers you would like me to deal with?

_____ 10. What is the nature of the population your organization serves?

_____ 11. _____

_____ 12. _____

_____ 13. _____

_____ 14. _____

_____ 15. _____

At the end of the interview, you may ask questions about the next steps you can expect, such as "What will the next step in your hiring process be?" or "When may I expect to hear from you again?" Either of these questions shows interest in the job and a desire on your part to continue the process.

Turn Nervous Energy into Positive Energy

A number of people who have recently started new jobs were asked about their experiences in the job interview process. Every single one of them said that he or she was nervous. However, each of them had also found a way to use the nervous energy or to control it.

Here are some of the answers that the successful job applicants gave:

> I know I need rest. I need to relax physically. The day before an interview, I didn't run around shopping. I went home, read the paper, and got a good night's sleep.

> I just focus on getting there. Then I walk to the interview. That gets rid of a lot of tension.

> I go through a lot of normal stuff like before a test. I try to plan the interview in my mind, think of the questions I might be asked. Also, dressing well makes me feel confident.

> I rely on thinking of the actor's saying. It's something like, "If you're nervous before you go on stage, you won't be nervous on stage and if you're not nervous before you go on stage, you're in trouble." I really just let the nervousness happen. All the nervousness beforehand gets you prepared, psyched.

> I use a little meditation and visualization. I picture myself being calm and having an easy flowing conversation with another human being.

You may have some ways you already use to help yourself in tension-producing situations. If you want to learn more techniques for doing this, read the book *Creative Visualization* by Shakti Gawain. If you want more information about how to use these techniques specifically for interviews as well as more information on all of the interview preparation steps, read *How to Have a Winning Job Interview.*

Track the Results of Your Interviews

Just as you kept track of your résumé mailings, you will want to keep track of the results of your interviews. The interview tracking records, like the résumé tracking records, should be saved to keep track of the possibilities in your job hunt. In fact, you can use the same index card or looseleaf system, stapling the interview tracking records to the matching résumé tracking records.

The interview tracking records can be used to be sure you have all the information you need when you set up an appointment for an interview. In many cases, the person who will interview you is not part of a personnel department, and the secretary calling you is not particularly familiar with making arrangements for an employment interview. You must take the responsibility for getting the information you need. In addition, it can be so exciting when the call for an interview comes that it is difficult to remember all your needs during the call. Make copies of the interview tracking records, keep them handy, and use them when you get calls.

A final use for the interview tracking records is to help you remember questions you were asked and help you analyze how to reply to similar questions in the future. While you don't want to be in a position of always second guessing yourself, it is helpful to reflect realistically on your own performance. It is likely that you will find that similar questions are asked by many different potential employers. In addition, the higher the job you are seeking, the more interviews you may have by different people in the same organization, and even there you will hear similar questions.

Interview Tracking Records

Name of organization _____

Street address _____

Room number _____

Date _____

Travel directions _____

_____

Name and title of interviewer _____

Person making arrangements _____

Telephone number _____

Materials to bring _____

Additional notes _____

Other people I met _____

Results of interview _____

_____

Next steps _____

_____

Most important question _____

_____

Most unexpected question _____

_____

My best answer _____

_____

Answer I would most like to change _____

_____

Extra Tips for a Winning Interview

Tip 1: *Plan your appearance as carefully as you plan your answers.* Neatness counts. Appropriateness counts. Moderation is the keynote. Be sure to wear clothes that make you feel good about yourself.

Tip 2: *Do not use jargon and abbreviations.* Most companies have their own vocabulary made up of company words and abbreviations. Avoid using these in an interview. Don't talk about OTPS and POs. Talk about a budget for supplies and services and purchase orders.

Tip 3: *Do not use jokes to answer questions.* One employer remembered a candidate who was in front of a panel interview. The candidate was asked, "What do you expect from your secretary?" She said, "Tender loving care." The secretary was on the panel. The candidate did not get the job.

Tip 4: *Do not be negative about your previous or present job or company.* That company and job will go on without you. Negativity creates the impression that you do not take responsibility for what you do. It also makes the interviewer side with your previous company and worry about your ability to get along in general.

Tip 5: *Do not know it all.* One of the employers said the worst thing is when a candidate says, "They didn't know how to run their business. I could really have improved things for them." This creates the impression that you will be judgmental about any company and will not be a good team player.

Tip 6: *Do not allow wrong impressions to remain.* If the interviewer has really misunderstood something you have said or has incorrect facts about you, politely correct her or him. Say "I believe I was not completely clear when I explained my last job. Although I did some selling, I was the sales manager, not one of the salespeople."

Tip 7:   *Listening is the key to a winning interview.* You let people know you are listening to them by facing them and maintaining eye contact. One of the most important reasons for listening to the interviewer is to hear the question. People who don't listen, who are jumping ahead in their minds to answers to questions they have not heard, do not do well in interviews. Not only do they fail to provide the information requested but they come across as poor communicators, as being "out of it." A major part of listening is not interrupting. Sometimes it is hard to tell if the interviewer has finished speaking, or is just pausing to gather thoughts, or breathe. Generally, you can tell by watching the person. If the interviewer turns to you or looks at you, a response is probably called for. On the other hand, if the interviewer is looking into the distance or down at the desk, it is probably just a pause in speech.

Summary Worksheet

This chapter took you through seven steps to a winning interview and then gave you seven extra tips. Look over the checklist below to be sure you have worked on each of the seven steps.

_____ I have thought about my strengths and my weaknesses.

_____ I understand the requirements of the job I am looking for.

_____ I know how my skills and knowledge meet the job requirements.

_____ I am familiar with the organization I am going to interview with.

_____ I have thought about how I can fit into the organization.

_____ I know the kinds of questions to expect and some ways to answer them.

_____ I know what is important to me in the job I am seeking, and I know which questions to ask and when to ask them.

_____ I know how to use my nervous energy.

_____ I have planned what I will wear to the interview.

_____ I have prepared interview tracking records.

_____ I have looked over my completed interview tracking records to remind myself of key questions and good answers.

How to Make the Right Career Moves—A Final Word

Each person's career is a unique path of education, experiences, decisions, and external circumstances. Although this book can give you some guidelines on asking questions and making moves in your career, only you can decide which are the right career moves for you.

Part of the decision regarding which career moves are right for you is based on what is most important to you. Some people gain satisfaction from the amount of money they earn. Others find that the amount of time they have for independent action is the most important value to them. Still others are not happy in their job unless it has some element of service to others. The values you hold dear will play a large part in determining the career path you choose to follow. In fact, you may find that the values important to you at one stage of your life shift in importance as you grow older.

Another aspect of the decisions that go into your making the right career moves are the interests that you have. Some people prefer to work with numbers, others with words, and still others with things. You may prefer to work closely with other people or to be on your own. You may like loosely structured situations or prefer highly ordered ones. Furthermore, none of these interests stand alone. They are held in combinations that are unique to you and work along with your values, your abilities, and your knowledge to suggest different directions for your career.

All of this means that you are the final judge of the rightness of any career move. If you ask for advice from friends or family, they generally give it in terms of their own values and perhaps in terms of their own interests and abilities. Many people feel that the only way to move in a career is up, and they narrowly define up to mean earning more money and reaching the next rung on a predetermined career ladder. The right direction for you at any given career decision-making point can be up, across, out, or even what others might consider down.

So the first rule of making the right career moves is the old adage "Know thyself."

Of course career moves are not made in a vacuum. There is the reality of the job market and business conditions. You can be prepared to make the right career moves by staying aware of current conditions. Read newspapers and current periodicals. Be aware of conditions in your organization and the industry at large. Join a professional association. Attend professional meetings and seminars related to your field. Read professional journals or newsletters.

The job market itself does not exist outside the society. Trends toward global markets and operations and technological advances affect all fields. Look for opportunities to increase your knowledge. Enroll in courses either in degree or nondegree programs. Look for seminars and workshops that can increase your specific skills or general knowledge. Take advantage of company policies to pay for increased education.

The world changes, industries change, businesses are created and closed. Even if you choose never to make a change, it is unlikely that your job will remain the same from the beginning of your work life to its end. Coping with a changing world means having flexibility, adaptability, the willingness to change within an occupation and within an organization.

Seek satisfaction from work. When you have figured out what makes you tick—what gives you satisfaction—see how you can find it in your current job. If you recognize that you cannot get that satisfaction, then plan to move on. The key word in that last sentence is *plan*. To get greater satisfaction, you need to have a plan. An effective plan will begin with an analysis of what you want. It will then move to where you can find it, and it will end with how you can get it. It is hoped that this book was helpful and will be helpful in the three stages of that planning. At any of these stages, do not be reluctant to seek help from professional sources if you need it.

When you decide to move—across, out, on another path, up—recognize that you may very well experience frustration. Studies of people in the process of changing directions in their careers show that often there is a period of difficulty and even unhappiness during the change. However, other studies also show that those who are unhappy or dissatisfied but do not change experience the greater despair.

Do not be afraid to dream. There is no end to the dreams you can use to set challenges for yourself and no age at which you must stop dreaming. If you choose a less traditional path or make a career move at an age that is unusual, you may find some greater hurdles to overcome, but you will also find some unexpected sources of strength and support.

The book *Peak Performers* (Avon Books) analyzed the accomplishments and career paths of over a thousand very successful people. The subjects of the book were people who had used their abilities to the fullest. The most important characteristics found by the author of the book have been turned into statements in the checklist that follows. Use this final checklist to see how you can be a peak performer.

Peak Performance Checklist

_____ I have a purpose in my life.

_____ I have formulated plans to reach my goals.

_____ If I feel trapped in my work, I am ready to move on.

_____ Before I take a risk, I examine the consequences, but I am willing to take risks.

_____ I feel self-confident because I know my past success came about through my skills and abilities.

_____ When something goes wrong, I am not interested in who is to blame. I just try to solve the problem.

_____ I use visualizations to imagine positive outcomes to future events.

_____ I like to take control of situations.

_____ The quality of my work is important to me.

_____ I know how to work with others around me and can often help them improve their work.

APPENDIX A: Consumer Guidelines for Selecting a Career Counselor

Sometimes it seems that virtually everyone is a vocational coach, ready and anxious to give advice, suggestions, and directions. Unfortunately, all are not equally able to provide the kind of help persons need in making decisions about what to do with their lives. Promises and luxurious trappings are poor substitutes for competency. Thus, the selection of a professional career counselor is a very important task. The following guidelines are offered to assist you in making this selection.

Credentials of the Professional Career Counselor

A nationally certified career counselor signifies that the career counselor has achieved the highest certification in the profession. Further, it means that the career counselor has:

141

- earned a graduate degree in counseling or in a related professional field from a regionally accredited higher education institution

- completed supervised counseling experience that included career counseling

- acquired a minimum of three years of full-time career development work experience

- obtained written endorsements of competence in career counseling from a work supervisor and a professional colleague

- successfully completed a knowledge-based certification examination

Other professional counselors may be trained in one- or two-year counselor preparation programs with specialties in career counseling and may be licensed or certified by national or state professional associations.

What Do Career Counselors Do?

The services of career counselors differ, depending on competence. A professional or nationally certified career counselor helps people make decisions and plans related to life/career directions. The strategies and techniques are tailored to the specific needs of the person seeking help. It is likely that the career counselor will do one or more of the following:

- conduct individual and group personal counseling sessions to help clarify life/career goals

- administer and interpret tests and inventories to assess abilities and interest and to identify career options

- encourage exploratory activities through assignments and planning experiences

- utilize career planning systems and occupational information systems to help individuals better understand the world of work

- provide opportunities for improving decision-making skills

- assist in developing individualized career plans

- teach job-hunting strategies and skills and assist in the development of résumés

- help resolve potential personal conflicts on the job through practice in human relations skills

- assist in understanding the integration of work and other life roles

- provide support for persons experiencing job stress, job loss, career transition

Ask for a detailed explanation of services (career counseling, testing, employment search strategy planning, and résumé writing). Make sure you understand the service and your degree of involvement and financial commitment.

Fees Select a counselor who is professionally trained and will let you choose the services you desire. Make certain you can terminate the services at any time, paying only for services rendered.

Promises Be skeptical of services that make promises of more money, better jobs, résumés that get speedy results, or an immediate solution to career problems.

Ethical Practices A professional or nationally certified career counselor is expected to follow ethical guidelines of such organizations as the National Career Development Association, the American Association for Counseling and Development, and the American Psychological Association. Professional codes of ethics advise against grandiose guarantees and promises, exorbitant fees, and breaches of confidentiality, among other things. You may wish to ask for a detailed explanation of services offered, your financial and time commitments, and a copy of the ethical guidelines used by the career counselor you are considering.

These guidelines were produced by the National Career Development Association and are reprinted with their permission.

APPENDIX B:
Related Readings

The books and publications mentioned in *How to Make the Right Career Moves* are listed below as sources of additional information.

Readings Related to Job Satisfaction

Modern Man in Search of a Soul. C. G. Jung. Trans. by W. S. Dell and Cary F. Baynes. New York: Harcourt Brace Jovanovich, originally published 1933.

The Motivation to Work. Frederick Herzberg, Bernard Mausner, and Barbara B. Snyderman. New York: John Wiley & Sons, Inc., 1959.

Peak Performers. C. Garfield. New York: Avon Books, 1986.

Sweet Death, Kind Death. Amanda Cross. New York: E. P. Dutton, Inc., 1984.

Work and Motivation. Victor H. Vroom. New York: John Wiley and Sons, Inc., 1964.

Writing a Woman's Life. Carolyn G. Heilbrun. New York: W. W. Norton and Company, 1988.

Readings Related to Information about Occupations and Industries

Periodicals

Business Week

ComputerWorld (This is an example of a weekly newspaper for one field. Other fields may have newspapers or journals as well.)

New York Times

Wall Street Journal

Working Woman

Books

Employment Policies: Looking to the Year 2000, National Alliance of Business, 1986.

A Job Search Handbook for Educators. Association of School, College and University Staffing, Inc., 1989. (This is an example of a publication of a professional association. Other associations may be able to provide additional materials.)

Occupational Outlook Handbook. U.S. Bureau of Labor Statistics, updated biennially.

Opportunities in Insurance Careers. Robert Schrayer. Lincolnwood, Ill: VGM Career Horizons, 1987. (There are many others in this series about individual careers such as *Opportunities in High Tech Careers* and *Opportunities in Cable Television.)*

Reference works *Bottin International Register*

Dun and Bradstreet's Million Dollar Directory

Fraser's Canadian-Trade Directory

Standard & Poor's Register of Corporations, Directors and Executives

Thomas Register of American Manufacturers

Readings Related to Job-Seeking Skills *Creative Visualization.* Shakti Gawain. New York: Bantam Books, 1979.

How to Have a Winning Job Interview. Deborah Perlmutter Bloch. Lincolnwood, Ill.: VGM Career Horizons, 1987.

How to Write a Winning Résumé. Deborah Perlmutter Bloch. Lincolnwood, Ill.: VGM Career Horizons, 1989.

VGM CAREER BOOKS

OPPORTUNITIES IN
*Available in both paperback and
hardbound editions*
Accounting Careers
Acting Careers
Advertising Careers
Aerospace Careers
Agriculture Careers
Airline Careers
Animal and Pet Care
Appraising Valuation Science
Architecture
Automotive Service
Banking
Beauty Culture
Biological Sciences
Biotechnology Careers
Book Publishing Careers
Broadcasting Careers
Building Construction Trades
Business Communication Careers
Business Management
Cable Television
Carpentry Careers
Chemical Engineering
Chemistry Careers
Child Care Careers
Chiropractic Health Care
Civil Engineering Careers
Commercial Art and Graphic Design
Computer Aided Design and Computer
  Aided Mfg.
Computer Maintenance Careers
Computer Science Careers
Counseling & Development
Crafts Careers
Culinary Careers
Dance
Data Processing Careers
Dental Care
Drafting Careers
Electrical Trades
Electronic and Electrical Engineering
Energy Careers
Engineering Careers
Engineering Technology Careers
Environmental Careers
Eye Care Careers
Fashion Careers
Fast Food Careers
Federal Government Careers
Film Careers
Financial Careers
Fire Protection Services
Fitness Careers
Food Services
Foreign Language Careers
Forestry Careers
Gerontology Careers
Government Service
Graphic Communications
Health and Medical Careers
High Tech Careers
Home Economics Careers
Hospital Administration
Hotel & Motel Management
Human Resources Management Careers

Industrial Design
Information Systems Careers
Insurance Careers
Interior Design
International Business
Journalism Careers
Landscape Architecture
Laser Technology
Law Careers
Law Enforcement and Criminal Justice
Library and Information Science
Machine Trades
Magazine Publishing Careers
Management
Marine & Maritime Careers
Marketing Careers
Materials Science
Mechanical Engineering
Medical Technology Careers
Microelectronics
Military Careers
Modeling Careers
Music Careers
Newspaper Publishing Careers
Nursing Careers
Nutrition Careers
Occupational Therapy Careers
Office Occupations
Opticianry
Optometry
Packaging Science
Paralegal Careers
Paramedical Careers
Part-time & Summer Jobs
Performing Arts Careers
Petroleum Careers
Pharmacy Careers
Photography
Physical Therapy Careers
Physician Careers
Plumbing & Pipe Fitting
Podiatric Medicine
Printing Careers
Property Management Careers
Psychiatry
Psychology
Public Health Careers
Public Relations Careers
Purchasing Careers
Real Estate
Recreation and Leisure
Refrigeration and Air Conditioning
  Trades
Religious Service
Restaurant Careers
Retailing
Robotics Careers
Sales Careers
Sales & Marketing
Secretarial Careers
Securities Industry
Social Science Careers
Social Work Careers
Speech-Language Pathology Careers
Sports & Athletics
Sports Medicine
State and Local Government

Teaching Careers
Technical Communications
Telecommunications
Television and Video Careers
Theatrical Design & Production
Transportation Careers
Travel Careers
Veterinary Medicine Careers
Vocational and Technical Careers
Welding Careers
Word Processing
Writing Careers
Your Own Service Business

CAREERS IN
Accounting
Advertising
Business
Communications
Computers
Education
Engineering
Health Care
Science

CAREER DIRECTORIES
Careers Encyclopedia
Occupational Outlook Handbook

CAREER PLANNING
Admissions Guide to Selective
  Business Schools
Career Planning and Development for
  College Students and Recent Graduates
Careers Checklists
Careers for Bookworms and
  Other Literary Types
Careers for Sports Nuts
Handbook of Business and
  Management Careers
Handbook of Scientific and
  Technical Careers
How to Change Your Career
How to Get and Get Ahead
  On Your First Job
How to Get People to Do Things Your
  Way
How to Have a Winning Job Interview
How to Land a Better Job
How to Make the Right Career Moves
How to Prepare for College
How to Run Your Own Home Business
How to Write a Winning Résumé
Joyce Lain Kennedy's Career Book
Life Plan
Planning Your Career of Tomorrow
Planning Your College Education
Planning Your Military Career
Planning Your Young Child's Education

SURVIVAL GUIDES
Dropping Out or Hanging In
High School Survival Guide
College Survival Guide

VGM Career Horizons
A Division of National Textbook Company
4255 West Touhy Avenue
Lincolnwood, Illinois 60646-1975 U.S.A.